2-28-22

ALTERNATIVE F@CTS

FAKE NEWS, TWEETS & THE 2016 ELECTION

WILLIAM GOODSPEED

Published by Satirical Press International
Copyright © 2017, Satirical Press International, William Goodspeed
https://williamgoodspeed.com/
All rights reserved.

ISBN-13: 978-0-9988853-0-8
Ebook ISBN: 978-0-9988853-1-5
Library of Congress Control Number: 2017905038
Cover design by: Katie Bielawski fantabulousdesign.com
Cover illustration by: Craig B. Campbell
Interior design & production by: Charlotte Cromwell

Conceived, Written, Laughed About, Designed and
Printed in the United States of America

1 2 3 4 5 6 7 8 9 10

The articles in Alternative Facts are entirely fictional, and the public
figures depicted therein are for satire. All other persons named in the articles are
fictional. All Tweets from public figures are, however, real.

Photographs under license from Shutterstock or from colleagues and author,
including the photos of Starbucks iced coffee and a McDonald's sign.
Both are trademarks of excellent companies and products.

Typeset in Adobe Garamond, Avenir, and Tiny Hand.

Tiny Hand is a new font created by Mark Davis and
is inspired by Donald Trump's handwriting.
"The font's name is a reference to an insult first levied at Trump 30 years ago by Vanity
Fair magazine editor Graydon Carter, who famously referred to Trump as a "short-fingered
vulgarian." Trump's Republican opponent Marco Rubio brought this insult back into the
limelight after criticizing the businessman's hands once again on his campaign trail, with
Trump refuting these insults on a number of occasions."
-Paul Tamburro

Dedication

Alternative Facts is dedicated to the members of the 2016 Falmouth High School Girls' Tennis Team. On a bus ride to a match, I promised that if they won the Maine State Championship, I would dedicate my book to them, as well as incorporate their youthful lingo. Their response: "We're super stoked to, like, help. Your book is so dope, bro."

They eventually won the state title,
so here's a shout out to the state champs*:

*Julia, Caroline, Annie, Kate, Amanda,
Mary, Mia, Grace* and *MJ.*

*To my darling three daughters (Anna, Merrill and Ellie) and three step daughters (Molly, Elizabeth and Sam), the next one's for you!

I would like to extend special thanks to Jenny Green and Kathy Fisher of Fisher Green Creative, LLC, who encouraged me to write this book and were instrumental in its design.

TRiGGER WARNiNG

Alternative Facts is a satire about the American Election of 2016. As such, it contains <u>fictional</u> accounts of public figures, including political figures and national journalists (all non-public figures are fictional). If you don't understand satire or are offended by ideas contrary to your political leanings, avoid reading this book while operating heavy machinery.

Alternative Facts does, however, contain hundreds of actual Tweets from political candidates, as well as real quotes. The author reviewed thousands of Tweets from 2015, 2016 and 2017 to provide real comments related to the topics of satirical articles and stories.

In addition, the book contains verbatim Facebook responses to the satires. If you need to understand the election, look no further than the enlightening Facebook comments (note: the horrible grammar, spelling and occasional vulgar language in the comments are not the author's) and the number of 'likes' of candidate Tweets.

The Tweets and Facebook copies in this work are intended to provide context and meaning to the satires expressed in the blogs under *Satirical Press International.*

ONe

Regular 'Mericans:
Clinton Road Trips to Iowa in Van
April 2015

Hillary Clinton ✔
@HillaryClinton

Road trip! Loaded the van & set off for IA. Met a great family when we stopped this afternoon.
Many more to come. -H

2 Apr 2015

Satirical Press International — Democratic Presidential Frontrunner and Former Secretary of State, Hillary Clinton, sat in her Chappaqua, New York home on a cool April afternoon with one of her longtime aides. They were finishing a bottle of nice 2004 French Bordeaux.

Mrs. Clinton turned to her aide and said, "You know what?"

"What's that, Madame Secretary?"

"The 2004 is every bit as good as the 2002. I should never have doubted you."

"Good to hear. Sorry again that we ran out of the 2002."

"Don't mention it. Hey, you know what would be great?" Madame Secretary asked.

"If Donald Trump ran for President and won the Republican nomination? We'd be in like Flynn!" the aide replied.

"The Republicans may be bat-shit crazy, but they're not that crazy."

"What would be great, Madame Secretary?"

"Why don't we go on a road trip?"

"Now?"

"Why not? I don't have a job now. It'd be fun. We could rent a Scooby-Doo van, get a cooler, some finger foods, and I have this great playlist on my iPhone. We could just drive and sing songs."

"Where would we go?"

"I dunno. Let's just get in the car and head somewhere random. Maybe Iowa?"

"Good a place as any. Could we stop at McDonald's?"

"Yes! It would be good to be seen there."

"Goodie. I always crave a Big Mac and fries after drinking Bordeaux."

"I prefer brie and grapes."

"Madame Secretary, you are amazing."

"How so?" Clinton asked.

"A former First Lady, United States Senator and Secretary of State and yet you really are a common person, totally down-to-earth. Imagine, a spontaneous road trip and even going to McDonald's," the aide pointed out.

"Shucks. I'm just an ordinary gal — I don't have to travel by private jet all the time."

"You really are a woman of the people."

"By the way, does McDonald's serve French wines?"

Hillary Clinton ✔
@HillaryClinton

Bye for now, Iowa, & thank you! I loved talking to so many of you about what's on your mind & your ideas for the future. See you soon! -H

12:24 PM 16 Apr 2015

162 replies 530 retweets 1,763 likes

POST-INAUGURATION POST SCRIPT:

The Bad News: Secretary Clinton's efforts to be a woman of the people hit a snag when her quarter million dollar speeches to Goldman Sachs, and her husband's $17 million consulting contracts, came to light.

The Good News: Secretary Clinton learned how to handle self-serve gasoline for the first time and became a fan of Quarter Pounders with Cheese and McDonald's fries (who isn't?).

TWO

Trump Announces Presidential Run, 'The Apprentice' Panics
June 2015

 Donald J. Trump ✔
@realDonaldTrump

To all my fans, sorry I couldn't do The Apprentice any longer – but equal time (presidential run) prohibits me from doing so. Love!

9:39 AM - 14 Sep 2015

708 replies 1,179 retweets 3,867 likes

Satirical Press International — The political world was abuzz today as real estate mogul, casino owner and Apprentice star Donald J. Trump announced his intention to run for the office of President of the United States. In a well-choreographed move, Mr. Trump and his wife, Melania, descended on an escalator in Trump Tower while the tune, Rockin' in the Free World, blared.

"It was unbelievable," commented a tourist named Doris from Kansas, who was visiting Trump Tower. "I mean, just as Mr. and Mrs. Trump decide to come downstairs, the song Rockin' in the Free World kicks in really loud. It was a sign from above!"

A male reporter from NBC News, who had heard rumors of an announcement and hustled up Fifth Avenue, witnessed the event and was interviewed by Anderson Cooper of CNN: "It was amazing — a thing of beauty. I couldn't stop staring."

"Donald Trump was that awesome?" Cooper inquired.

"Donald Trump? Oh, I didn't notice him. I was referring to Melania."

After the escalator ride, Mr. Trump assumed the podium with a backdrop of American flags and spoke to the gathering crowd, including Doris.

"He talked about how America had gone wrong, how we needed better deals," Doris explained. "I didn't know what was coming, but then he said America needed a leader who wrote 'Art of the Deal', and that narrowed it down a bit for me."

By most counts, the Trump speech was uplifting. Mr. Trump talked about how America needed a cheerleader, a positive force, and that President Obama was no cheerleader. He said America needed "someone who can take the brand of the U.S. around the world and make it great again."

"Politicians are usually so negative, so critical," Doris explained to CNN. "It's so refreshing to have someone so positive, so chivalrous running for President this time. The world is gonna love Mr. Trump!"

Not everyone was happy with the event, like NBC. Mr. Trump's run for President means he can no longer star on the NBC show, The Apprentice. As Mr. Trump noted, "The Apprentice is the number one show on television," but he would have to give it up.

An executive for NBC, who wished to remain anonymous, said, "It's true. The Apprentice is number one, not counting the 66 shows ranked ahead of it."

Asked who would replace Mr. Trump on the show, the executive said, "We're working on it, but Dick Cheney is lookin' pretty good."

POST-INAUGURATION POST SCRIPT:

A few weeks into President Trump's term, the author tried to reach Doris from Kansas to see how she felt about the President's positivity and the new brand of the U.S. overseas. Apparently, the millions who protested after the inauguration, both home and abroad, were unaware of the positive branding efforts.

Also, Trump's successor on The Apprentice was Arnold Schwarzenegger. Mr. Trump's initial praise soured a bit once the former California Governor took over:

Donald J. Trump ✓
@realDonaldTrump

Congrats to my friend @Schwarzenegger who is doing next season's Celebrity Apprentice. He'll be great & will raise lots of $ for charity.

9:39 AM - 14 Sep 2015

396 replies   2,291 retweets   4,337 likes

Donald J. Trump ✓
@realDonaldTrump

Wow, the ratings are in and Arnold Schwarzenegger got "swamped" (or destroyed) by comparison to the ratings machine, DJT. So much for....

4:34 AM - 6 Jan 2017

17,621 replies   9,527 retweets   39,791 likes

Donald J. Trump ✓
@realDonaldTrump

Yes, Arnold Schwarzenegger did a really bad job as Governor of California and even worse on the Apprentice...but at least he tried hard!

3:24 AM - 3 Feb 2017

28,345 replies   24,023 retweets   119,264 likes

THREE

Megyn Kelly, Rosie O'Donnell Hammered in First Republican Debate
August 2015

Donald J. Trump ✓
@realDonaldTrump

I really enjoyed the debate tonight even though the @FoxNews trio, especially @megynkelly, was not very good or professional!

12:53 AM - 7 Aug 2015 from Manhattan, NY

1,587 replies 3,821 retweets 9,425 likes

Donald J. Trump ✓
@realDonaldTrump

Sorry, @Rosie is a mentally sick woman, a bully, a dummy and, above all, a loser. Other than that she is just wonderful!

5:53 PM - 8 Dec 2014

227 replies 919 retweets 1,310 likes

Satirical Press International — The race for the Republican Nomination for the 45th President of the United States got off to bang last night at the first Republican debate in Cleveland, Ohio. The event was hosted by Fox News and watched by 24 million Americans.

"Incredible ratings, no surprise, none at all," Republican frontrunner, Donald Trump said, "I'm the reason why."

Fox News had hoped that the loyal viewers who made The Apprentice the 67th most popular show on television would follow Mr. Trump to the debate, and they were not disappointed--the viewing audience was much higher than expected.

"It was great theater tonight," exclaimed a Fox executive. "Ten Republican candidates in a bloody free-for-all to make their mark without getting torched by Mr. Trump. We're thinking about making this a killer reality TV show."

Other networks conducted focus groups to understand viewer reaction to the event. NBC's group, moderated by Lester Holt, displayed a diverse reaction to the Republicans' performance. One participant, Norm, a truck driver from Pittsburgh wearing a tee shirt that said "Kick Ass and Take Names" with an American flag, summed up the view of many viewers:

"Trump don't take shit from no one, Lester. He tells it like it is; people like Rosie O'Donnell should be on noticed." After Mr. Holt asked how he felt about Mr. Trump's manner in the debate, Norm said, "We need tough, confident people who beat the livin' shit out of everyone. No more mamby pambies Muslims like Barack Hussein Obama. No makin' omelets without crackin a few eggs."

If Trump was the big winner of the night, the big losers were comedian Rosie O'Donnell and Fox News moderator Megyn Kelly. In response to a question from Kelly about referring to women as 'fat pigs', Mr. Trump said, "Only Rosie O'Donnell."

When Ms. Kelly corrected Mr. Trump to say he had insulted many more women than the Hollywood star, Trump said, "I've been really nice to you, but I could not be based on the way you treated me." Tension between Mr. Trump and Ms. Kelly seemed palpable and will likely spill over past the debate.

About this, Norm added: "She's just another liberal media person."

Holt reminded him that Ms. Kelly works for Fox News, a notoriously conservative outfit.

"The only fair media is Rush Limbaugh. The rest is all a bunch a commies," Norm said.

Donald J. Trump ✓
@realDonaldTrump

I liked The Kelly File much better without @megynkelly. Perhaps she could take another eleven day unscheduled vacation!

6:50 PM - 24 Aug 2015 from Manhattan, NY

1,693 replies 2,754 retweets 5,371 likes

Donald J. Trump ✓
@realDonaldTrump

Do you ever notice that lightweight @megynkelly constantly goes after me but when I hit back it is totally sexist. She is highly overrated!

7:00 PM - 22 Sep 2015 from Manhattan, NY

1,531 replies 2,730 retweets 6,649 likes

Donald J. Trump ✓
@realDonaldTrump

I refuse to call Megyn Kelly a bimbo, because that would not be politically correct. Instead I will only call her a lightweight reporter!

3:44 AM - 27 Jan 2016

5,490 replies 7,166 retweets 19,830 likes

Donald J. Trump ✅
@realDonaldTrump

Why does @megynkelly devote so much time on her shows to me, almost always negative? Without me her ratings would tank. Get a life Megyn!

7:58 PM - 16 Feb 2016

2,852 replies 4,895 retweets 14,377 likes

Hillary Clinton ✅
@HillaryClinton

What Trump said about Megyn Kelly is outrageous—but what's really outrageous is Republicans' actual positions on issues that affect women.

2:33 PM - 10 Aug 2015

589 replies 2,147 retweets 4,026 likes

Donald J. Trump ✅
@realDonaldTrump

Meryl Streep, one of the most over-rated actresses in Hollywood, doesn't know me but attacked last night at the Golden Globes. She is a.....

3:27 AM - 9 Jan 2017
71,508 replies 38,358 retweets 125,497 likes

POST-INAUGURATION POST SCRIPT:

No one would have imagined Fox News to be singled out as biased against Mr. Trump, but it happened. Mr. Trump accused Megyn Kelly of having blood coming out of her 'everywhere', boycotted the next Fox Debate to raise money for veterans, and eventually chased Ms. Kelly away from Fox to NBC News, a notoriously left-wing network. President Trump has not let up on celebrities, taking on Meryl Streep and asserting she is overrated.

And when it comes to Rosie and President Trump, it's fair to say their mutual feelings have not diminished.

FOUR

First Democratic Debate: Sanders Puts Clinton Email Controversy to Rest
October 2015

Donald J. Trump ✔
@realDonaldTrump

At the request of many, and even though I expect it to be a very boring two hours, I will be covering the Democrat Debate live on twitter!

2:43 AM - 13 Oct 2015

1,330 replies 4,347 retweets 8,053 likes

Satirical Press International — The Democratic Party staged the first of its debates last night in Las Vegas, Nevada with almost 16 million Americans watching on television. As expected, the largest conflict in the debate was between Democratic frontrunner, Secretary Hillary Clinton, and Vermont Senator, Bernie Sanders.

Since Secretary Clinton is such a known commodity, focus group moderators were keen to see how Americans reacted to the relatively unknown Senator Sanders. In a focus group in Des Moines, Iowa, home of the first Democratic caucus, reactions to Mr. Sanders were mixed. One man, Floyd, a sixty-five year-old from Pella, said, "I had never heard Senator Sanders before. He kinda reminds me of those old guys on The Muppet Show — you know — the crazy ones in the balcony making cat calls."

15

A sophomore from Iowa State in nearby Ames, Bethany, had this to say about the former socialist: "I like the way he talks with his hands. It's so, like, super cool. I'm also super stoked about getting free college since I have, like, two more years, not counting grad school in body massage."

The big winner of the night appeared to be Secretary Clinton for a very unexpected reason. During a heated exchange, Senator Sanders thundered, "Secretary Clinton, we're all sick to death of hearing about your damn emails!" Co-moderator Anderson Cooper from CNN had this to say about the remark: "Senator Sanders showed a lot of grace tonight about the emails. It looks like the email cloud following the Secretary may have lifted for good."

But others say the biggest winner was Republican frontrunner Donald Trump, who Tweeted throughout the debate, frequently commenting on the poor quality of the set, the boring participants and the frequency of commercials. The Trump Tweets got more attention than the debate at times. His most impactful debate Tweet concerned Russian President, Vladimir Putin:

Donald J. Trump ✔
@realDonaldTrump

Putin is not feeling too nervous or scared. #DemDebate

5:45 PM - 13 Oct 2015

1,129 replies 3,760 retweets 7,720 likes

As a result of this Tweet, the popularity of Mr. Trump soared among Americans. "Mr. Putin is a very bad man — a killer," explained a woman from Joliet, Illinois. "We need a president who sees right through him and stands up to his shenanigans. Trump is the one!"

Donald J. Trump ✔
@realDonaldTrump

@BernieSanders-who blew his campaign when he gave Hillary a pass on her e-mail crime, said that I feel wages in America are too high. Lie!

8:49 AM - 27 Dec 2015

1,776 replies   1,949 retweets   5,061 likes

POST-INAUGURATION POST SCRIPT:

As it turned out, Senator Sanders may have been alone in being sick of Secretary Clinton's damn emails, as the issue dogged her until Election Day. But the biggest surprise was that instead of being tough on Putin, Mr. Trump continually praised him. One observer noted: "I've only heard President Trump praise four people: himself, General 'Mad Dog' Mattis, Dr. Martin Luther King Jr. (who is dead) and Vladimir Putin. It's an interesting mix of folks."

Five

Third Republican Debate:
Leaders Attack Science, Media
October 2015

 Ben & Candy Carson ✔
@RealBenCarson

It is important to remember that amateurs built the Ark and it was the professionals that built the Titanic. @my_ccu

29 Oct 2015

 Donald J. Trump ✔
@realDonaldTrump

After a great evening and packed auditorium in Iowa, I am now in Colorado looking forward to what I am sure will be a very unfair debate!

7:53 AM · 28 Oct 2015

1,262 replies   1,617 retweets   4,121 likes

Satirical Press International — Many expected the Third Republican debate, which took place in Republican stronghold Boulder, Colorado, to be a continuation of the rise of Carly Fiorina, former CEO of Hewlett Packard, over criticism of her looks. Instead, 14 million Americans watched what many now call 'The Greatest Blow on Earth', and they were not disappointed.

However, it wasn't frontrunner Donald Trump who dominated the airwaves, but Dr. Ben Carson, a retired pediatric neurosurgeon from Detroit. The usually highly subdued candidate went nuclear over vaccination: "Almost all children get vaccinated, and a certain small number get autism, and so if you look at it and don't pay attention to logic, you might say all children with autism have been vaccinated."

"You're really passionate about this, aren't you, Dr. Carson?" asked CNBC moderator Becky Quick.

"This really gets my blood boiling," Carson added in a monotone.

"I can see that. Do you consider yourself a man of science, Dr. Carson?"

"Absolutely. I'm a pediatric neurosurgeon, trained at Yale."

"Do you believe in climate change?" Quick asked.

"Just look around you. The climate changes every day. Some days are hot, and some are cold. And there is wind, rain and snow. It was very cool here in Boulder this morning. There is no doubt that things change."

"As a scientist, do you believe climate change is due to human influences?" Quick asked.

"I think your tone shows bias against Republicans, Ms. Quick."

"How so?"

"The media favors Secretary Clinton, and these debates are nothing more than a game of gotcha," Dr. Carson explained.

"I just asked if you believed people caused climate change," Ms. Quick tried to explain.

"It's a liberal question, another sign of bias in the East Coast arrogant media. You should ask scientists, and they don't agree."

"But 98% of scientists agree that humans are causing climate change.

What do you say to that?"

"As I Tweeted today, amateurs built the arc, but professionals built the Titanic."

"So we should not listen to professional scientists and facts?"

"We should listen to people with a different set of facts," Carson said.

"Interesting point of view," Quick retorted.

"It's much easier that way."

six

A Future Peek at the Muslim Ban
December 2015

"Donald J. Trump is calling for a total and complete shutdown of Muslims entering the United States until our country's representatives can figure out what is going on."

Trump Press Release, December 7, 2015

Satirical Press International — It's the spring of 2018, and former NBA great Kareem Abdul-Jabbar enters the immigration hall at Washington Dulles Airport after two weeks of cooking classes in Tuscany. In line, he strikes up conversation with Dr. Oz, the famous TV doctor, who was returning from an extended yoga seminar in Tibet. Waiting in line, they notice a large portrait of Donald Trump, the 45th President of the United States, on the wall. Dr. Oz said, "His color is returning to normal since the campaign. The orange made me think he was eating too many carrots."

When it's his turn, Mr. Abdul-Jabbar steps up to the immigration officer.

"What's your name?" the immigration officer asks.

"Kareem Abdul-Jabbar."

"Do you speak English, sir?"

"Yes, I graduated from UCLA."

"In LA?"

"Yes, sir, that's what the LA in UCLA stands for."

"No wonder. I hear there are a lot of camel jockeys in LA."

"I wouldn't know, sir."

"Take these forms and go to the special window over there."

"Why?"

"Because you have one of those Muslim names. If you had a real American name, like Lew Alcindor, you would stay in this line."

"What will they do to me over there?"

"Ask you questions to determine if you're Muslim."

"But I am Muslim, sir."

"Then it will be a quick interview, and they'll put you on a plane back home. President Trump's orders."

"Oh, no problem, sir."

"I must say, you're taking this better than most, Mr. Abdul-Jabbar."

"My home is LA, and that's where I'm going."

"No dice. LA may be full of illegal Mexicans, but it's still part of the U.S. NEXT!"

Kareem leaves for the Muslim-questioning window. Dr. Oz hands his passport, which showed his given name of Mehmet Öz, to the immigration agent.

The agent looks up and says, "Mehmet Öz?"

"Yes, sir."

"What kind of name is Öz?"

"Turkish."

"How'd you learn to speak English, Mr. Öz?"

"I went to college at Harvard and medical school at Penn, followed by an MBA at Penn also. I've lived and worked in the U.S. all my life."

"If I had a dollar for every time I've heard one of you desert nomads say that, I'd be retired. Do you have any proof of your claim?"

Looking in his wallet, Dr. Oz says, "I don't carry my diplomas with me, but here is my Applebee's card."

"Sorry, but we'll need more than that. If you're American, as you say, where do you go to church?"

"Church?"

"Yep. President Trump ordered us to ask. It's not that tough of a question, sir."

"But I don't go to church; I'm a Muslim."

"That's why we ask. Please step to the line over there."

Hillary Clinton ✓
@HillaryClinton

Donald Trump's anti-Muslim proposal is extreme – but not by the standards of the rest of the 2016 Republican field.

11:02 AM - 9 Dec 2015

329 replies 1,128 retweets 1,391 likes

Donald J. Trump ✔
@realDonaldTrump

The United Kingdom is trying hard to disguise their massive Muslim problem. Everybody is wise to what is happening, very sad! Be honest.

11:02 AM - 9 Dec 2015

329 replies   1,128 retweets   1,391 likes

Donald J. Trump ✔
@realDonaldTrump

Hillary Clinton said that it is O.K. to ban Muslims from Israel by building a WALL, but not O.K. to do so in the U.S. We must be vigilant!

5:23 AM - 2 Jan 2016

1,998 replies   7,737 retweets   14,402 likes

Donald J. Trump ✔
@realDonaldTrump

Incompetent Hillary, despite the horrible attack in Brussels today, wants borders to be weak and open-and let the Muslims flow in. No way!

7:59 PM - 22 Mar 2016

4,201 replies   13,187 retweets   36,190 likes

Donald J. Trump ✔
@realDonaldTrump

It is amazing how often I am right, only to be criticized by the media. Illegal immigration, take the oil, build the wall, Muslims, NATO!

7:38 AM - 24 Mar 2016

2,329 replies   7,308 retweets   21,736 likes

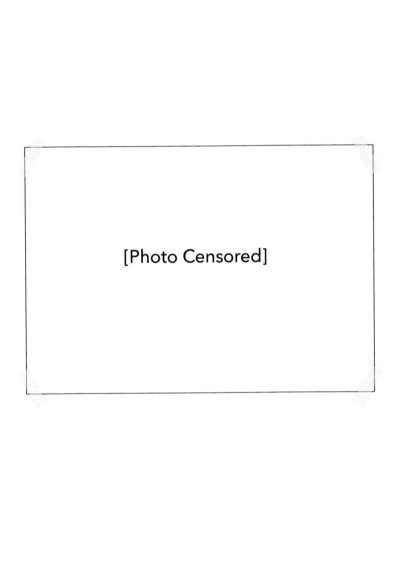

seven

Clinton Got 'Schlonged'
December 2015

"She (Clinton) was favored to win, and she got schlonged."
— Donald Trump.

Satirical Press International— Today, in a public statement, Republican Presidential Candidate Donald Trump said that Secretary Clinton had gotten 'schlonged' by Barack Obama in the 2008 Democratic Primaries. The use of this term caused outrage among English teachers across America.

Speaking from a high school in East Grand Rapids, Michigan, a woman English teacher in her seventies did not hold back her scorn: "This is a sign of the demise of proper English — schlong is a noun. We don't need politicians making verbs out of perfectly good nouns."

"Here, here," echoed an English teacher from Charlotte, North Carolina. "Mr. Trump should realize that children listen to his speech. Before long, we'll have more verbs than Spanish — and look what happened to them."

Others claimed that the term 'schlong', whether used as a noun or verb, refers to the male urinary and copulatory organ and has no place in public discourse.

"Bullshit!" responded a Trump Campaign spokesperson, "schlong is a perfectly acceptable word to describe total domination and defeat. Mr. Trump does not use offensive vulgarities. People who think schlong's offensive are just a bunch of pussies."

Former President Bill Clinton denounced the Trump statement during a rally in Iowa. He shook his finger and said, "President Obama never schlonged Hillary, not a single time."

 Donald J. Trump ✓
@realDonaldTrump

When I said that Hillary Clinton got schlonged by Obama, it meant got beaten badly. The media knows this. Often used word in politics!

7:37 PM - 22 Dec 2015

3,020 replies   10,113 retweets   17,619 likes

 Donald J. Trump ✓
@realDonaldTrump

Once again, #MSM is dishonest. "Schlonged" is not vulgar. When I said Hillary got "schlonged" that meant beaten badly.

4:47 PM - 22 Dec 2015

2,086 replies   4,168 retweets   7,404 likes

eiGHT

Clinton Edges Sanders by Cow Pie in Iowa Caucus
February 2016

 Hillary Clinton ✔
@HillaryClinton

Hillary just became the first woman ever to win the #IowaCaucus.

2:10 PM - 2 Feb 2016

379 replies 1,534 retweets 3,550 likes

Satirical Press International — On February 1, 2016, Secretary Hillary Clinton became the first woman ever to win the Iowa Caucus after trouncing Senator Bernie Sanders, 49.8% to 49.6%.

"Thank you, Iowa!" the pantsuit-clad Secretary bellowed in her usual, somewhat stilted style. "Tonight, the people of Iowa have spoken; it is a roar that is being heard around the world!"

When confronted with the fact that she won by only .2% of the vote, the Secretary shook it off. "The will of the people will not be denied!"

Asked how she pulled off her first win of the 2016 campaign, the Secretary said, "It all started last spring, when my assistant and I spontaneously road tripped from New York to Iowa in a Scooby Doo van. We sang songs, ate burgers, stopped at truck stops — my assistant even tried a little Redman. Before she got dizzy and retched into her McDonald's Diet Coke, she seemed to really enjoy it. By doing all these things, we showed Iowans that we are regular Americans, men and women of the soil, cut from the same cloth that they are, settlers on the Plains and all that. It was a trip full of discovery."

"What did you discover?" asked a reporter from the Des Moines Register.

"Did you know that you can swipe your credit card at a gas pump, and you don't even have to go inside?"

"That's amazing. Anything else?" asked the reporter.

"For some reason, the pickles on McDonald's burgers are really good. I can't get enough!"

"Amazing."

"And Dunkin Donuts has coffee."

"It's quite good."

"No kidding, and it was my first coffee in a paper cup. Yep, I'm just a regular dadgum gal."

In the Sanders camp, the mood was more somber. Addressing his dispirited campaign staff, the Vermont Senator said, "First, I must congratulate Secretary Clinton on her victory. She won fair and square."

Asked what he thought accounted for the .2% difference, the Senator said, "The van ride played a factor, certainly, but my staff thinks I made a strategic error."

"What was that?"

"I refused to throw cow pies at the Iowa State Fair."

New Hampshire Voter
Shows Appreciation for Science

NiNe

Trump, Sasquatch Big New Hampshire Winners
February 2016

Donald J. Trump ✔
@realDonaldTrump

Thank you, New Hampshire! Departing with my amazing family now! #FITN #NHPrimary

7:38 PM - 9 Feb 2016

Donald Trump Jr., Eric Trump, Lara Trump and 2 others

1,088 replies   4,162 retweets   14,304 likes

Satirical Press International — A week after finishing second in the Iowa Caucus, Republican candidate Donald Trump clobbered his Republican rivals to win the New Hampshire primary, the first in the interminable 2016 presidential election. The question many Americans are asking is: how can a casino and nightclub owner with vulgar language, orange skin, four bankruptcies, two divorces and the bedside manner of a python win a major primary?

To answer that question, The Satirical Press International, sent its political reporter, Denis Roy, to New Hampshire to investigate. What he found was truly amazing. Roy reported that many primary voters in New Hampshire were "a can short of a six pack." Proof came in a

New Hampshire parking lot where Roy found a car window sticker for the Sasquatch Field Research Team (see photo). The following is an excerpt from Roy's report: "It's beyond belief. I may sound arrogant accusing this car owner of stupidity, but doesn't everyone know that Sasquatch lives in the Northwest? They will never find Sasquatch in New Hampshire, no matter how hard they look. No wonder everyone's so frustrated and pissed off."

According to Roy, Donald Trump has been courting Sasquatch enthusiasts brilliantly, and he may take this theme all the way to Pennsylvania Avenue. Roy further reported: "Poor Jeb Bush just talks about immigration reform, national defense and the economy, topics certain to bore the typical voter. Kasich tries hard too, bringing sound fiscal policies and experience to bear, but he looks like he just rolled out of bed. Unfortunately, bed head doesn't appeal to primary voters, though it seems to work for Bernie Sanders, who easily won the Democratic Primary."

As a final note on the New Hampshire issue, Ted Cruz was temporarily delayed in traveling to campaign for the South Carolina Primary after being captured and tagged by the Sasquatch Field Research Team outside his NH campaign headquarters.

TeN

Canada to Build Wall
February 2016

 Donald J. Trump ✓
@realDonaldTrump

Mexico will pay for the wall!

3:31 AM - 1 Sep 2016

16,510 replies   36,623 retweets   62,405 likes

Satirical Press International — Canadians are no strangers to American politics, in large part because most live within an hour of the U.S. and watch CNN. The American primary campaigns in both parties started benignly for Canadians; most viewed it as entertainment. "It was more interesting than watching the mayor of Toronto get busted for smoking crack," chuckled one Canadian at a Toronto grocery store, "but then we started thinking, what if some of these American crazies won?"

As Donald Trump, Ted Cruz and Bernie Sanders rose improbably in the polls and won primaries, Canadians began worrying about a deluge of Americans crossing their border in 2017. "We watch CNN and see what they say," bemoaned a mother of three from Ottawa, "Americans are promising to flee to Canada in record numbers. I don't think we could handle it."

For this reason, newly elected Canadian Prime Minister Justin Trudeau announced a commission to study the possibility of erecting a wall on Canada's border with the U.S. "The key to this whole idea," explained Jay McKenzie, a spokesman for the Prime Minister, "is to build a wall high enough to keep out disgruntled Americans, but still allow Canadian geese to travel to America. We'd drown in goose shit if they're trapped here."

Wolf Blitzer, speaking from The Situation Room in CNN studios in Washington, asked Mr. McKenzie if they had enough information to design an effective wall. "Well, that's the $8 billion question, isn't it?"

"American or Canadian dollars?" asked the ever-inquisitive Mr. Blitzer.

"Whatever. It's a big number, but the problem is though we know a lot of people will be coming, we don't know who," explained Mr. McKenzie.

"By name?" asked Mr. Blitzer.

"No, I mean the type of person. What if Bernie Sanders wins? All these top .01% Americans will be packing up their penthouse apartments on Fifth Avenue and heading north for lower taxes in Canada."

"What difference would that make?" asked Blitzer.

"We can't build a wall to keep out all the private jets," snapped Mr. McKenzie. "Can you imagine? The tarmacs would be flooded with these planes, and French wine futures would skyrocket here. Heck, the run-of-the-mill Canadian millionaire won't be able to afford nannies anymore. It would be chaos."

Donald J. Trump ✓
@realDonaldTrump

FMR PRES of Mexico, Vicente Fox horribly used the F word when discussing the wall. He must apologize! If I did that there would be a uproar!

12:27 PM - 25 Feb 2016

5,651 replies   5,001 retweets   15,704 likes

Donald J. Trump ✓
@realDonaldTrump

Everyone is now saying how right I was with illegal immigration & the wall. After Paris, they're all on the bandwagon.

8:30 AM - 19 Nov 2015

1,279 replies 3,987 retweets 9,267 likes

Donald J. Trump ✓
@realDonaldTrump

Legal immigrants want border security. It is common sense. We must build a wall! Let's Make America Great Again!

12:06 PM - 11 Jul 2015

1,212 replies 3,412 retweets 4,649 likes

ELEVEN

Rubio, Trump Sent to Principal's Office
March 2016

"And you know what they say about men with small hands…"
– Marco Rubio Speech, February 29, 2016

Donald J. Trump ✓
@realDonaldTrump

Little Marco Rubio, the lightweight no show Senator from Florida, is set to be the "puppet" of the special interest Koch brothers.

8:07 AM - 28 Feb 2016

1,326 replies   3,674 retweets   9,668 likes

Satirical Press International — After hearing a deluge of Republican fighting and personal insults over the weekend, Harvest Elementary School Principal Margaret Schumacher summoned Donald Trump and Marco Rubio to her office. Mrs. Schumacher, a notoriously stern disciplinarian, welcomed the two Republican candidates into her office. Looking over her reading glasses, which had a string to hang around her neck, she peered at the presidential frontrunners. Rubio's upper lip was sweating profusely.

"You know why you're here, boys?" Mrs. Schumacher asked in a harsh tone.

"Of course. You're announcing that you are endorsing my campaign," Trump said.

"No, Donald. You two are in big trouble for fighting."

"He started it!" Rubio exclaimed, pointing at Trump.

"I did not!" Trump bellowed.

"Did too!"

"Quiet boys or there'll be no recess!" Schumacher shouted, "Let's get to the bottom of this, shall we?"

"Donald said I was sweating and using a towel to put on make up," Rubio said.

"Is that true, Donald?" Schumacher asked.

"No, I said trowel, and I only said it because he called me orange."

"Marco," Schumacher scolded, "We never, ever comment on student's skin color."

"But he keeps calling me 'little'," Rubio whined.

"You are little, and you're a baby too, nothing like the mobsters I deal with in business, and I've built a great business, believe me," Trump countered.

"You can't say that about fellow students, Donald, it's discriminatory."

Trump pointed at Rubio and shouted: "Then tell him to stop criticizing my hands!"

"What about his hands, Marco?" Schumacher asked.

"They're little."

Mrs. Schumacher looked at Trump's outstretched hand and said, "They are a bit small, Donald. Is it true what they say about men with small hands?"

"Are you kidding? I have a great body that does great things, better than anything little Marco or Obama can do, trust me. Ask any of my wives, any of them. And my body will continue to do great things in the White House, believe me."

"That's not fair!" Rubio barked. "Just because he says it doesn't make it true. Why does everyone believe him? He's got small hands. Let him show you his —"

"Not in front of me, boys!" Schumacher shouted. "Now get out of here and start acting like 11 year old boys should."

Donald J. Trump ✓
@realDonaldTrump

Lightweight Marco Rubio was working hard last night. The problem is, he is a choker, and once a choker, always a choker! Mr. Meltdown.

8:38 AM - 26 Feb 2016

3,503 replies 4,789 retweets 14,020 likes

Donald J. Trump ✓
@realDonaldTrump

Marco Rubio couldn't even respond properly to President Obama's State of the Union Speech without pouring sweat & chugging water. He choked!

7:37 PM - 9 Nov 2015

338 replies 1,168 retweets 2,654 likes

Donald J. Trump ✓
@realDonaldTrump

Word is-early voting in FL is very dishonest. Little Marco, his State Chairman, & their minions are working overtime-trying to rig the vote.

10:06 AM - 12 Mar 2016

2,211 replies 6,526 retweets 13,999 likes

TweLve

Romney, Trump Debate Hair Products
March 2016

"And I predict that despite his promise to do so, first made over a year ago, that he will never ever release his tax returns. Never – not the returns under audit; not even the returns that are no longer being audited. He has too much to hide."

Mitt Romney, March 1, 2016

 Donald J. Trump ✓
@realDonaldTrump

Mitt Romney, who was one of the dumbest and worst candidates in the history of Republican politics, is now pushing me on tax returns. Dope!

4:34 AM - 25 Feb 2016

4,417 replies   8,005 retweets   22,027 likes

Satirical Press International — In a first-ever event, Fox News hosted a debate between former and current Republican candidates for President. Anchor Megyn Kelly hosted the much-anticipated event in Detroit, Michigan, Mr. Romney's hometown. A huge, boisterous crowd greeted the candidates as they took the stage.

Ms. Kelly: "Good evening, Gentlemen."

Romney and Trump: "Good evening, Megyn."

Kelly: "Let's start with you, Mr. Romney. Today, you made a speech at the University of Utah. In the speech, you said Mr. Trump's promises were as worthless as a Trump University degree."

Romney: "That's right."

Kelly: "And you said Mr. Trump was not a good businessman, that he had inherited his business, had three bankruptcies and failed in numerous ventures, like Trump Airlines, Trump Vodka and Trump Steaks. Furthermore, you criticized Trump for praising Vladimir Putin and disparaging George W. Bush. You added that Trump acts like a bully, makes fun of disabled reporters and brilliant women."

Romney: "I think you got the gist."

Boos and cheers come from the crowd.

Kelly: "You've known Mr. Trump for some years; does he have any positive attributes?"

Romney: "No offense to you, Megyn, or my lovely wife, Ann, but let's be honest, Mr. Trump's wife, Melania, is stunning, and I might add, she's a successful immigrant."

Huge cheers from the crowd.

Trump: "Can we keep the discussion on important issues for the American people, Megyn?"

Kelly: "Like what?"

Trump: "Mitt Romney is a loser, a total choker. In 2012, he lost badly to a Muslim born in Kenya. He's even weaker than Little Marco."

Crowd erupts in cheers.

Kelly: "Mr. Romney?"

Romney: "Bullies notoriously overcompensate for their shortcomings."

Trump (*holding up his hands*): "Look at these hands, Megyn."

Huge cheers from the crowd.

Trump: "Do they look small to you? Believe me, I've got the whole package."

Delirious cheers erupt.

Kelly: "Are you actually alluding to male parts during a presidential debate on national TV?"

Romney: "Sounds like it to me. Is this the character we want in the White House?"

Trump: "You're just jealous, Slick Mitt, because my hair is better than yours. You have to compensate with gel. No wonder you're still married to the same woman."

Crowd: "U.S.A.! U.S.A.! U.S.A.!"

 Donald J. Trump ✔
@realDonaldTrump

Failed presidential candidate Mitt Romney, the man who "choked" and let us all down, is now endorsing Lyin' Ted Cruz. This is good for me!

1:18 PM - 18 Mar 2016

2,418 replies   5,747 retweets   20,855 likes

Donald J. Trump ✓
@realDonaldTrump

Mitt Romney had his chance to beat a failed president but he choked like a dog. Now he calls me racist-but I am least racist person there is

4:18 AM - 11 Jun 2016

7,407 replies   10,680 retweets   33,167 likes

Donald J. Trump ✓
@realDonaldTrump

Pocahontas is at it again! Goofy Elizabeth Warren, one of the least productive U.S. Senators, has a nasty mouth. Hope she is V.P. choice.

5:07 AM - 10 Jun 2016

6,747 replies   9,353 retweets   28,894 likes

THIRTEEN

Clinton Leather Dress Scandal
Mars Super Tuesday
March 2016

Satirical Press International — The day after Hillary Clinton's astounding victories in Super Tuesday, CNN anchor Wolf Blitzer is in The Situation Room. The CNN music for Breaking News interrupts his interview of Bernie Sanders' wife.

"Excuse me, Mrs. Sanders, but we are hearing some incredible breaking news about the Clinton campaign. For this incredible, potentially game-breaking news, let's go to our political correspondent, Pamela Brown, at Chick Fil-A headquarters in Atlanta."

(Pamela Brown nods seriously to the camera during the introduction with a large dairy cow standing next to her).

Brown: "Wolf, on the heels of Secretary Clinton's convincing victories yesterday, there is a new Clinton dress scandal developing."

Blitzer: "Can you share the details? What are you hearing? Does it have anything to do with Monica Lewinsky?"

Brown: "I'm here with Elsie, the famous Chick Fil-A spokescow who is known for her relentless campaign to reduce beef consumption. Today, she reported that her co-spokescow, Betsy, disappeared a week ago."

Turning to Elsie, Ms. Brown says, "Elsie, can you tell us what happened?"

Elsie: "Last week, Betsy went on her usual Starbucks run and no one has seen her since."

Blitzer interrupts: "Pamela, can you ask Elsie what Betsy had at Starbucks?"

Elsie: "I don't see how that's relevant, but she had a muffin and a soy Frappuccino®"

Blitzer: "Soy? Did you say soy? Isn't soy an unusual choice, especially for a dairy cow?"

Elsie: "It's, like, super creepy for us to have milk. It'd be like you drinking from a woman's — you know."

Blitzer continues: "Did Betsy have any enemies? Has she ever received any threats?"

Elsie: "Specifically, no, but she gives Ruth's Cris Steak House® a wide berth."

Blitzer: "Are you suggesting Ruth's did her in?"

Elsie: "We suspected it until we saw Hillary Clinton's leather dress last Friday night."

Blitzer: "What about her dress? Was there something unusual about it? How is it linked to Betsy? Does former President Bill Clinton have anything to do with it?"

Elsie: "She wore a new black and white leather dress to a campaign rally (*sniffle*); it was definitely Betsy's pattern. We're waiting on DNA confirmation."

Blitzer: "Why would Secretary Clinton do it? What's her motivation?"

Elsie (*sobbing*): "Because she can. She hangs with all those fat cats on

Wall Street and gives speeches to Goldman Sachs for a quarter-million dollars. Why settle for milk when you can have the whole cow?"

Blitzer to Brown: "Pamela, what are the ramifications of this for the Clinton campaign?"

Brown: "It's a big slap in the face to Bernie Sanders and the Vermont Ben 'n Jerry's granola crowd, that's for sure."

Blitzer: "Are there any policy implications associated with Mrs. Clinton's dress?"

Brown: "We've asked the Clinton campaign. They say this clearly shows there are no sacred cows — except the teachers' unions and Wall Street."

Blitzer: "From an historical perspective, if Secretary Clinton is elected, what does it mean? Is there any precedent?"

Brown: "She would be the first president to wear leather in office since Teddy Roosevelt and his chaps, though there are some rumors about the Kennedy years."

FOURTEEN

Obama Withdraws Garland Nomination, Taps Rush Limbaugh
March 2016

Donald J. Trump ✓
@realDonaldTrump

Rush Limbaugh is great, tells it as he sees it – really honorable guy! Thanks Rush! #Trump2016

3:49 PM - 22 Jan 2016

493 replies   1,858 retweets   5,689 likes

Satirical Press International — In a stunning announcement today at a White House news conference, President Obama withdrew his nomination of Merrick Garland for Supreme Court Justice. Mr. Obama said, "Though Mr. Garland is the Chief Justice of the most important Federal Appeals Court, former prosecutor of the Oklahoma City bomber and the Unabomber, valedictorian of his Harvard college class and distinguished graduate of the Harvard Law School, we have found, upon further review, that he is not qualified to serve on the Supreme Court."

CNN's Wolf Blitzer asked the President: "Mr. President, why did you withdraw your nomination of Mr. Garland less than a week after you made it? Did you find someone better? Did some compromising picture appear of Mr. Garland with another woman? Will you let the people decide?"

President Obama: "Thanks, Wolf, for your — um — question. It became clear to me that Mr. Garland was not suitable for the position when he cried during the announcement."

Blitzer: "How important was the crying? Did your vetting of Mr. Garland fail to reveal crying? Are you bowing to political pressure from Senate Republicans?"

President Obama: "Wolf, we're thinking about limiting reporters to one question per question, but anyway, Americans want strength in office. There's no crying in baseball or the Supreme Court."

Blitzer: "Do you have someone else in mind to nominate? Will he or she be more palatable to the Republicans? Is crying now an important disqualifier?"

President Obama: "In fact, yes. Today, I'm pleasured to announce my nomination for the next associate justice of the Supreme Court, Rush Limbaugh."

Later that day, Fox News' Megyn Kelly interviewed Senate Majority Leader Mitch McConnell about the Limbaugh nomination.

Kelly: "Senator McConnell, you have repeatedly said that the Senate will not even consider an Obama nomination, that it's up to the people to decide in the next election. Does the nomination of Rush Limbaugh change your position?"

McConnell: "Leave it to President Obama to try to pull a fast one on the American people and embarrass the Senate. This is just politics as usual in Washington. Once we state we will not act, he nominates the perfect candidate for the Court. No wonder no one will have a drink with him."

Kelly: "So you're in favor of Mr. Limbaugh?"

McConnell: "Absolutely. The people have spoken and pressured Mr. Obama to pull his unqualified candidate and nominate someone the people support."

Kelly: "Do you know that Mr. Limbaugh never went to law school?"

McConnell: "The Constitution does not require our Supreme Court justices to be lawyers. Law school in overrated, just a prop for the East Coast so-called intellectual elite."

Kelly: "In fact, Mr. Limbaugh never graduated from college and is a recovered drug user. He's also been married four times."

McConnell: "Mr. Limbaugh is a beacon of American values. The people are tired of Ivy League snobs in Washington."

Kelly: "So what's the next step in the process?"

McConnell: "We hold hearings in the Judiciary Committee and then vote in the Senate."

Kelly: "What about the senators who complained about being too busy for hearings?"

McConnell: "They'll just have to suck it up and make sacrifices, just like I am."

Kelly: "What sacrifices are you making?"

McConnell: "I have to cancel my participation in something I've been preparing for over many years — next month's Mr. Congeniality Contest in Atlantic City."

Donald J. Trump ✔
@realDonaldTrump

I wonder if President Obama would have attended the funeral of Justice Scalia if it were held in a Mosque? Very sad that he did not go!

8:42 AM - 20 Feb 2016

5,514 replies   12,188 retweets   29,438 likes

Facebook Comments to Article:

████████████ Rush would make a great press secretary for Trump.
Like · Reply · Message · March 22, 2016 at 11:18am

██████████████████████ Garland was the "white" patsy. Wasn't expected to be chosen. Who is next? Probably a Muslim.
Like · Reply · Message · March 22, 2016 at 1:54pm

FiFTeeN

Poll: Kasich Unqualified for Prez
March 2016

 Donald J. Trump ✓
@realDonaldTrump

Once John Kasich announced he was running for president, and opened his mouth, people realized he was a complete & total dud!

5:47 PM - 19 Nov 2015

477 replies 1,471 retweets 3,981 likes

Satirical Press International — CNN's Wolf Blitzer interrupts his interview of a Donald Trump spokesman for breaking news:

Blitzer: "We've just learned the results of a new CNN national poll. According to a poll of likely Republican voters, most do not believe Ohio Governor John Kasich is qualified to be President of the United States. For a full report, let's go to CNN's Chief Political Correspondent, Dana Bash, who is in Akron covering the upcoming Ohio primary."

(Bash slowly nods repeatedly to camera while Blitzer introduces her.)

Blitzer: Dana, what can you tell us about this incredibly important poll, maybe the most critical poll in this campaign, if not the last several elections?

Bash: Wolf, I just talked with Kasich campaign officials, and they can't make heads or tails of this.

Blitzer: Can you shed any light on the poll? Do Americans think Governor Kasich lacks the relevant experience of the other candidates or is it a character issue or maybe voters don't understand the Governor's record? Or was it something the other candidates did?

Bash: Great question, Wolf. I've gathered three likely Republican voters here for their views.

(*Three Ohioans stand next to Bash, who turns to interview middle-aged man wearing a Trump Make America Great Again hat*)

Bash: Sir, you are a Trump supporter, correct?

Man: Yes.

Bash: Let me share some facts with you: John Kasich has completely turned around Ohio's budget, from a huge deficit to a surplus, and he's been reelected and is a hugely popular governor.

Man: Yeah, so?

Bash: And he was in Congress for 18 years previously, elected in his early 30s and served as the head of the House Budget Committee, where he successful drafted a balanced budget, unheard of these days, and he was a member of the Armed Services Committee, making him quite knowledgeable of foreign and military affairs.

Man: If you say so.

Bash: Do you believe the Governor lacks the qualifications to be President?

Man: I just don't see how that liberal mumbo jumbo is relevant.

(*Bash turns to a young man in an Ohio State sweatshirt*)

Bash: In addition to what I just mentioned, do you know that Governor

Kasich graduated from Ohio State?

Young Man: Just because he went to The Ohio State University doesn't make him qualified. If we want a Buckeye, I would go with Urban Meyer, the football coach.

Bash: Why?

Young Man: Because he won the national championship with a third string quarterback; he'd make Mexico pay for the wall, no doubt.

(*Bash turns to middle-aged woman*)

Bash: Ma'am, after what I just said about Governor Kasich's qualifications, could you support him for President?

Woman: Until Donald Trump starts mocking him and calling him names, I just can't take him seriously.

 Donald J. Trump ✔
@realDonaldTrump

Ohio is losing jobs to Mexico, now losing Ford (and many others). Kasich is weak on illegal immigration. We need strong borders now!

8:03 AM - 15 Mar 2016

1,332 replies   5,371 retweets   16,118 likes

 Donald J. Trump ✔
@realDonaldTrump

Going to Ohio, home of one of the worst presidential candidates in history – Kasich. Can't debate, loves #ObamaCare – dummy!

2:11 PM - 23 Nov 2015

828 replies   2,497 retweets   6,321 likes

SIXTEEN

Castro Brothers to Trump: Reinstate Cuban Embargo *Rapidamente!*
March 2016

Satirical Press International — At a welcome reception for President Obama and his family at the seat of the Cuban government in Havana, El Capitolio, Fidel and Raúl Castro shared a moment with the American president over strong mojitos with limes in a private chamber.

Fidel: "*Bienvenidos a Cuba, Señor Presidente!*"

Obama: "Thank you, *Señores Castro.* It's great to be here, and may I say, these *mojitos* with lime are very strong."

Raúl: "Where is your military uniform, *Señor Presidente?*"

Obama: "We don't wear uniforms. I am a civilian."

Fidel: "What? Then how did you become leader of America?"

Obama: "I was elected — twice."

Raúl: "How much longer will you be in power, *Señor Presidente?*"

Obama: "Until next January. May have another *mojito* please?"

Fidel: "*Señor Presidente,* I suggest you take the limes out of your glass. People are counting and starting to talk."

Raúl: "Next January? Do you have a brother who will take over?"

Obama: "No, we have elections in November. Do you have a big plate or something where I can put all these limes?"

Fidel: "Just use the waste bin here and put some napkins over them. I learned that trick a long time ago."

Raúl: "Elections? Does the Party vote on the next president?"

Obama: "No, every citizen over 18 years old can vote."

Raúl: "Very peculiar and dangerous. Is that what all the fuss is about? I keep seeing this man with strange hair and orange skin talking — he always seems — how do Americans say — pissing off?"

Obama: "Pissed off. Yes, that's Donald Trump, who will likely be the Republican nominee."

Fidel: "Is there something the matter with his hands? I heard *Señor Rubio* talk about it on CNN International."

Obama: "CNN? You have cable? Do you get ESPN here?"

Fidel: "Is *Señor Trump* on ESPN today?"

Obama: "No, I'm trying to see how my NCAA basketball bracket is doing. Do you know if Oklahoma won yesterday?"

Raúl to one of his security men: "Please find out if Oklahoma won."

Obama: "And while you're at it, could you check on Oregon too?"

Raúl: "Of course."

Obama: "Man, these mojitos are *bueno*."

Raúl: "Back to this election, *Señor Presidente*. This *Señor Trump* says some crazy things about Latinos and great deals, incredible deals, deals like no Americans have seen."

Obama: "He's stoked about deals." To a waiter while pointing to his *mojito*: "Could you please top this off?"

Raúl: "Could he win this thing you call an election?"

Obama: "It's quite possible. He'll be running against Hillary Clinton, who has some legal problems, so you never know."

Deep in thought, **Raúl** says: "*Señor Presidente,* we are very concerned about this *Señor Trump* and his deals. Is it possible for you to reinstate the embargo?"

Donald J. Trump ✔
@realDonaldTrump

Fidel Castro is dead!

5:08 AM - 26 Nov 2016

27,830 replies 99,458 retweets 209,810 likes

Donald J. Trump ✔
@realDonaldTrump

If Cuba is unwilling to make a better deal for the Cuban people, the Cuban/American people and the U.S. as a whole, I will terminate deal.

6:02 AM - 28 Nov 2016

10,256 replies 24,565 retweets 84,395 likes

SEVENTEEN

Trump Launches 'Your Momma' Attacks
March 2016

Donald J. Trump ✓
@realDonaldTrump

How can Ted Cruz be an Evangelical Christian when he lies so much and is so dishonest?

4:03 AM - 12 Feb 2016

2,909 replies   4,884 retweets   11,903 likes

Satirical Press International — It's 5:10 p.m. in the CNN Situation Room. The music for Breaking News blares and alerts viewers to upcoming news. Wolf Blitzer comes on air and can barely control his excitement:

"We interrupt CNN coverage of the bird that landed on Bernie Sander's podium to bring you breaking news on the Republican campaign for President. For this, we go to CNN Political Correspondent Pamela Brown outside the Trump mansion in Palm Beach, Florida. Pamela, what say you?"

Brown nods repeatedly with a microphone and announces: "Wolf, I'm here outside the Trump mansion in Florida with a major development. The Trump campaign is no longer ridiculing Ted Cruz's wife, and is now going all out against his mother."

Wolf sits forward in his chair in excitement: "His mother? What about his mother? Is this about whether she was actually a U.S. citizen when Senator Cruz was born in Canada? Or is there another issue with Mrs. Cruz?"

Brown: "All good questions, Wolf. Let me address one at a time. At a press conference this morning, Donald Trump launched a scathing personal attack on her character and preference in men."

Blitzer: "What kind of attack? Are the Cruz children in any way involved?"

Brown: "Trump said to Senator Cruz: 'Your momma wears army boots and swims out to meet troop ships.'"

Blitzer: "What kind of boots? Are they American army boots or Cuban? Or maybe Canadian? And what country are the troop ships from? Is this a statement against our troops?"

Brown: "He did not specify, but he also said to Cruz: 'Your momma is so ugly that when she watches TV, the channels change themselves.'"

Blitzer: "What channels? Are there any particular programs that change themselves?"

Brown: "The channels aren't relevant. The point is . . ."

Blitzer: "Hold on a minute, Pamela. We are now getting a report from Cruz headquarters in Houston from Dana Bash. Dana, what can you tell us about the TV channel controversy?"

Bash: "Wolf, a spokesman for Senator Cruz said the comment about the senator's mother is blatantly false — she rarely wears army boots and never swims to troop ships, even American ones."

Blitzer: "So these unprecedented charges are false? Fake news, if you will."

Bash: "Senator Cruz just made the following statement: 'The Donald's accusations of my momma's army boots, troop ship visits and TV stations changing are complete fabrications. He is in a bad place to criticize. To him I say, Donald your momma was so ugly, she didn't need a costume for a part in the Star Wars bar scene.'"

Blitzer: "Dana, do you know what character Mrs. Trump played in the Star Wars bar scene? Was she part of the band?"

Bash: "We called the Star Wars Producer George Lucas about the bar scene accusation. He couldn't remember exactly but thought she may have been the green horn player."

Blitzer: "Thanks, Dana. We're eagerly awaiting confirmation of the Star Wars story. Now back to Palm Beach where Donald Trump is launching a new round of 'Your Momma' attacks. Later, if time permits, we will cover today's arrest of three terrorist suspects in Belgium."

 Donald J. Trump ✓
@realDonaldTrump

I don't think Ted Cruz can even run for President until he can assure Republican voters that being born in Canada is not a problem. Doubt!

5:57 PM - 18 Jan 2016

1,349 replies   2,054 retweets   5,975 likes

 Donald J. Trump ✓
@realDonaldTrump

It's time for Ted Cruz to either settle his problem with the FACT that he was born in Canada and was a citizen of Canada, or get out of race

5:26 AM - 25 Jan 2016

1,310 replies   2,788 retweets   7,513 likes

Donald J. Trump ✔
@realDonaldTrump

Wow, Lyin' Ted Cruz really went wacko today. Made all sorts of crazy charges. Can't function under pressure - not very presidential. Sad!

4:02 PM - 3 May 2016

2,849 replies 7,906 retweets 24,926 likes

Facebook Comments to Article:

████████ Hay guys I don't give a dam what your mom are wife's did r didn't do get back on what the hell u are going to do for the poor people

Like · Reply · Message · March 28, 2016 at 8:59pm

eiGHTeeN

7% Of White Men Aren't Pissed Off
March 2016

Satirical Press International — At the NBC Today Show studios at 30 Rockefeller Center, Host Matt Lauer announces: "The rise of Donald Trump and Bernie Sanders in the 2016 election defies expectation, and despite their seemingly opposite stances, they have a common thread of voter anger, particularly among white men. Well, we now have an explanation. In news breaking overnight, an NBC/Quinnipiac poll has determined that only 7% of white American men are actually not angry. To explain this phenomenon, let's go to Savannah Guthrie on location in Denver, Colorado. Good morning, Savannah. What do you have for us?"

"Matt, good morning. Since news broke about the shocking poll, we've been searching high and low for white men who aren't angry."

"It looks like you found a few."

"Yes, Matt, I'm here with three white men who told me they aren't pissed off at all."

Turning to the first, Ms. Guthrie asks: "Good morning. You are Jay Newman, a 35-year old software engineer from right here in Denver, correct?"

Newman: "That's right, Savannah. Good morning."

Guthrie: "Can you confirm that you're not an angry white male?"

Newman: "You got it. I've got a great job, a new Prius, and I'm happy."

Guthrie: "What do you say to those who say immigration is ruining America, particularly Latinos?"

Newmark: "Two words, Savannah — Sophia Vergara."

Guthrie: "Say no more. I'm a big Modern Family fan myself. Let's go next to Mr. Sean Murphy. Can you tell the folks something about yourself, Sean?"

Murphy, who has scraggly hair and a soul patch under his lower lip: "I'm, like, a 25 year old in my 7th year of a comparative religion major at Colorado Boulder — Go Buffs, bro."

Guthrie: "7 years seems like a long time to be in college, Sean."

Murphy: "The snow has been, like, super sweet for boarding the past few years, Bro, so I don't, like, take many classes in the winter. And the marijuana legalization has been super cool, but it slowed me down."

Guthrie: "So it's true you aren't angry?"

Murphy: "No, Bro. Since college became free, I've been, like, super chill."

Guthrie: "But college isn't free. Bernie Sanders hasn't been elected."

Murphy: "No (beep)! Maybe I'm a little angry after all. Wanna brownie?"

Guthrie: "Um, no thanks. Let's go to our last happy male, Mr. Bobby Gaston from Fort Collins, a 50-year old construction worker. Mr. Gaston, why in the world are you not mad?"

Gaston: "This is America, Savannah, the land of opportunity. We have-what? — 30 NFL teams, and all the non-expansion teams have been to the Super Bowl at least once, except the Lions and Browns. It's amazing. Where else in the world could that happen?"

Guthrie: "I can't think of a single country, thanks. Back to you in New York, Matt."

Lauer: "Thanks, Savannah. After this short break, a special report: What does your cat think about in the litter box?"

NINETEEN

Aliens Return Trump
April 1, 2016

Satirical Press International — Trump Tower, New York City, April 1, 2016.

Two thin green figures stand behind a podium in the lobby of Trump Tower. They resemble ET with green skin, bulging eyes, long fingers and extended necks. The taller of the two has a silver earring, soul patch under his lower lip and a black Bernie Sanders tee shirt. Dozens of reporters hold microphones and recording devices. Cameras flash incessantly, and news crews start filming.

Two identical Donald Trumps stand next to the podium, one on each side of the aliens.

Shorter Alien: "Good afternoon. Thank you for coming on such short notice. We are honored."

Taller Alien: "Yeah, kudos, bros."

Every reporter's hand urgently went up.

Shorter Alien: "I'm sure you have many questions for Mr. Trump, but before we get to those, I'd like to read a prepared statement. (He puts on reading glasses and opens a folder and reads). Exactly one year ago,

April 1, 2015, my friend here and I, who hail from a star cluster on the far side of the Milky Way in case you're interested, decided to play a small April Fools' prank on the United States."

Shorter Alien continuing: "We decided to abduct Donald Trump and replace him with a near exact double."

Taller Alien: "It, like, got out of hand, dudes."

Shorter Alien: "As you can see, we replicated the hair perfectly."

Taller Alien: "But we shrunk his hands so we could, like, tell them apart."

Shorter Alien: "We programmed the Trump replacement to run for president and say unbelievable things."

Taller Alien: "Like building a wall to keep out aliens, bros. That's hilarious."

Shorter Alien: "Due to a software programming glitch, the second Trump said increasingly disturbing things. It started to scare a lot of people, like Megyn Kelly of Fox News . . ."

Taller Alien: "And Canadians, man."

Shorter Alien: "Anyway, the prank went a little too far, so today, we're bringing back the real Donald Trump, as you can see. Well.....that's it for the prepared remarks, any questions?"

All hands went up and the reporters shouted.

New York Times reporter **David Brooks**: "Where did you learn to speak English?"

Shorter Alien: "University of Phoenix on line."

Taller Alien: "Snowboarding in Vail, dude."

CNN's Carole Costello: "What do you think about the movie, ET?"

Taller Alien: "Totally rad, bro. I, like, cried at the end and tried to phone home."

NBC's Lester Holt: "Can you shed any light on the strange patterns and shapes that show up in wheat fields?"

Taller Alien: "I got this one, bro. My friend here and I went to Cancun to learn about spring break and discovered tequila a few years ago, man. We, like, don't have that stuff at home. So we got lit one night and took the spaceship out to do donuts in wheat fields."

MSNBC's Joe Scarborough: "What're your favorite things about America?"

Taller Alien: "I'd have to say the rice bowls at Chipotle, dude."

Shorter Alien: "Jennifer Anniston."

NBC's Matt Lauer: "Any plans while you're in New York?"

Shorter Alien: "I've always wanted to see Cats."

Katie Couric: "What are you going to do with the Trump double?"

Taller Alien: "Take him home and fix the glitch, man."

POST-INAUGURATION POST SCRIPT:

At least one reader claimed this article was fake.

Photos by Nick Forester, Falmouth High School Class of 2019

TWENTY

Making (in China) America Great Again
April 2016

Satirical Press International — In the run up to the pivotal Republican Wisconsin Primary, Donald Trump appears on Fox News' America Live with Megyn Kelly. Mr. Trump appears in a dark blue suit with red tie hanging well below his belt buckle, sitting across from Fox's blonde rising star.

Kelly: "Mr. Trump, many in the media say last week was your worst yet as a candidate after a precocious high school freshman in Maine broke the story that your 'Make America Great Again' hats are made in China. If you look at the monitors, you'll see pictures of a hat with a shipping label from Shenzhen, China. What do you say to that?"

Trump (*raising his hand and right index finger*): "First, that's not a very nice question. We have far more delegates than anyone else and are doing great things, amazing things, even though the RNC is attacking me, which quite frankly is very offensive."

Kelly: "With all the talk about China stealing our jobs, how do you explain going to China to produce your red hats?"

Trump: "China didn't steal those jobs from America — the Chinese stole the jobs from the Mexicans, so by buying our hats from China, we're undermining the Mexicans and showing them we mean business, and by the way, I'm a great businessman who does great deals."

Kelly: "So by outsourcing production of hats to China, you're actually helping American workers? I'm sorry, but I don't understand that at all."

Trump: "That's because you're a blonde ditz, not that all blondes are ditzes. I love blondes and get along great with them, and they love me. Two of my wives were blonde, and they were beautiful, beautiful women, believe me, not like Heidi Cruz or Hillary Clinton."

Kelly: "Mr. Trump, there are those who say you never take accountability for mistakes."

Trump: "That's not a very nice question, Megyn. If I made mistakes, I would consider taking accountability for them, but I don't make mistakes. I have a big brain and went to Wharton."

Kelly: "So you don't take accountability for not being accountable?"

Trump: "I'm not going to answer a hypothetical question."

Kelly: "Have you ever apologized for something?"

Trump: "I have nothing to apologize for."

Kelly: "After your campaign manager got arrested for battery against a woman reporter last week, you can't find something to say you're sorry for?"

Trump: "On second thought, I can."

Kelly: "What?"

Trump: "I'm sorry you're a loser."

Kelly: "Well, that's a start."

Trump: "I'm just getting started, believe me."

Kelly: "What else?"

Trump: "You're a bimbo who didn't get into Wharton, and you're not very nice."

Kelly: "Quite an endorsement. Any last words, Mr. Trump?"

Trump (*holding up his hands*): "Take a look at these hands, will you?"

TWENTY-ONE

Sanders Ups Stakes: Free Beer!
April 2016

Bernie Sanders ✓
@BernieSanders

Public colleges and universities tuition free? Damn right.

7:37 PM - 14 Apr 2016

331 replies 6,660 retweets 12,799 likes

Donald J. Trump ✓
@realDonaldTrump

Strange, but I see wacko Bernie Sanders allies coming over to me because I'm lowering taxes, while he will double & triple them, a disaster!

5:34 AM - 28 Dec 2015

1,907 replies 3,927 retweets 9,589 likes

Satirical Press International — CNN's Wolf Blitzer is in the Situation Room.

Blitzer: "We have some incredible news breaking from the Bernie Sanders campaign. As the battle for the New York Democratic Primary heats up, Bernie Sanders has issued a new policy paper. For this, we go to New York to talk to the Senator directly."

Blitzer: "Good afternoon, Senator Sanders."

Sanders: "Thanks for having me, Wolf."

Blitzer: "Senator, what is the new domestic policy you are proposing? Does this have anything to do with Secretary Clinton's claim that you are not qualified to be President? What is the mood like in the campaign? Are you optimistic about the New York Primary?"

Sanders: "Wolf, I'm having a little trouble with my ear piece. I lost you after the third question."

Blitzer: "I lose track myself sometimes. Anyway, what's the new policy?"

Sanders: "Like our elections, our economy is rigged. The billionaires are getting richer and everyone else is struggling. As you know, I'm backing a plan for free universal health care for all Americans as well as free college tuition for all. Today, I'm announcing a new plan to provide free beer to all adult Americans."

Blitzer: "Free beer? This is an unprecedented move and an incredible extension of your domestic agenda, possibly the most significant of your campaign."

Sanders: "The people have suffered long enough, Wolf."

Blitzer: "Will it be domestic or foreign beer? How does this square with your trade policy? Will Corona and Corona Light be included under NAFTA?"

Sanders: "Our plan will call for only domestic beer. Only Secretary Clinton and her billionaire friends would support Heineken or Corona."

Blitzer: "What about Americans who prefer wine? How will your policy handle them?"

Sanders (*raising both hands*): "Wine is the nectar of the damn billionaire class! It will not be covered under the policy."

Blitzer: "Even Three Buck Chuck?"

Sanders: "Even the damn Three Buck Chuck!"

Blitzer: "What about Americans who don't drink? What say you to them?"

Sanders: "Now would be a good time to start."

Blitzer: "Senator Sanders, our federal budget deficit is greater than $400 billion per year, and we have nearly $19 trillion of debt, and that's before free medical care and college tuition. How do you plan to pay for the beer?"

Sanders: "Three things. First, deficits don't really matter, and we'll significantly raise taxes on the billionaires and Secretary Clinton's Wall Street cronies. Second, the federal government will use its bargaining power to negotiate favorable prices, and third, we will only offer Busch Light."

Blitzer: "Skeptics will say your policy favors millennials and northern states — older voters prefer craft brews and southern NASCAR fans love Bud Light Lime. Is this just a stunt to shore up your base?"

Sanders: "Busch Light is our damn national beer, not for the billionaire class! — every college kid in America drinks it!"

Blitzer: "Thanks, Senator Sanders. Let's go to Clinton headquarters for a response to the free beer policy."

Donald J. Trump ✔
@realDonaldTrump

How is Bernie Sanders going to defend our country if he can't even defend his own microphone? Very sad!

1:23 PM - 22 Aug 2015 from New Jersey, USA

1,642 replies   5,192 retweets   9,012 likes

Donald J. Trump ✔
@realDonaldTrump

Bernie Sanders endorsing Crooked Hillary Clinton is like
Occupy Wall Street endorsing Goldman Sachs.

10:01 AM - 12 Jul 2016

3,084 replies   35,653 retweets   51,543 likes

Facebook Comments to Article:

███████████ F*CK Sanders! & his free shit!

Like · Reply · Message · April 11, 2016 at 7:15pm

███████████ I'm beginning to think he's better at attacking than
the gop

Like · Reply · Message · April 11, 2016 at 10:33pm

███████████ what a frikin moron...free beer! What's next? Free
phones???

Like · Reply · Message · April 12, 2016 at 1:39am

William Goodspeed Teresa, maybe I should write about free
phones. Blackberry could sure use a lift. But anyway, this is just
poking fun through satire and exaggeration. I don't think Sanders
really promotes Busch Light.

Like · Reply · Message · April 12, 2016 at 8:50am

███████████ Vote Trump

Like · Reply · Message · April 12, 2016 at 10:15am

███████████ I'm gonna leave this hear for all to Read..

'Feeling the Bern' of Socialism . . . *See More*

Like · Reply · Message · April 12, 2016 at 10:34am

███████████ I'll take free beer any day of the week

Like · Reply · Message · April 12, 2016 at 12:25pm

William Goodspeed A man after my own heart, though I try to avoid Busch Light.

Like · Reply · Message · April 12, 2016 at 3:43pm

TWENTY-TWO

Candidate Jeopardy!
April 2016

Satirical Press International — On the set for the game show, Jeopardy, contestants Donald Trump, Ted Cruz and John Kasich each stand behind a podium with their handwritten names in front. Enter Alex Trebek, longtime star of the show.

Trebek *(looking at the camera)*: "Welcome tonight to a very special show featuring the three remaining Republican presidential candidates. Good evening gentlemen, and welcome. Let's play Jeopardy. The categories for Jeopardy are:

> *Clinton Scandals . . .*
>
> *The Bill of Rights . . .*
>
> *Waterboarding . . .*
>
> *Mexicans . . . and*
>
> *Convention Rules.*

Cruz smiles broadly: "Right in my wheelhouse, Alex."

Trebek: "Mr. Trump, you lead in the polls and will go first."

Trump: "Bill of Rights for $600."

Trebek: "Prevents police from breaking down your door."

Cruz buzzes in first: "What are handguns and semi-automatic rifles?"

Trebek: "No, sorry. Anyone else? . . . (buzzer sounds). What is the Fourth Amendment? Still your board, Mr. Trump."

Trump: "Bill of Rights for $800."

Trebek: "Taking the Fifth refers to this."

Cruz buzzes again: "What is a liquor store robbery?"

Trebek: "Sorry. (buzzer) What is right not to bear witness against oneself in the Fifth Amendment? Go again, Mr. Trump."

Trump: "Waterboarding for $1,000."

Trebek: "This vice president famously said it was not torture."

Trump: "Dick Cheney."

Trebek: "You must ask a question, Mr. Trump."

Trump: "I don't ask questions, Alec, I give answers, and I give good answers, believe me, really good answers, folks, because I have a good brain, and if you want better deals for American — and we've had really bad deals, horrible deals, like giving Iran $150 billion — I will make great deals, such good deals that America will get tired of —"

Trebek: "Wow, this is a long answer; let's take a commercial break for Aleve."

(*After the break*) **Trump continues:** "and we'll build a wall, folks, a big wall, believe me, and Mexico will be happy to pay for it, and we'll be tough on China — though I love the Chinese, many of my business colleagues are Chinese; they're a great people — I have many Muslim friends too, but until we figure this thing out, no Muslims will enter the U.S —"

Trebek: "Sorry, Mr. Trump. You're now at minus $1,000, but it's still your pick."

Trump: "Mexicans for $800."

Trebek: "And the answer is 122 million."

Trump: "The number of American jobs lost to illegal immigrants."

Trebek: "It needs to be in the form of a question. (buzzer). The question was: What is the population of Mexico?"

Trump: "Your facts are wrong. This game is rigged, like the Republican delegate system. If I have the most delegates — and I will, folks, the Republicans aren't going to give me the nomination? This is a democracy, folks, believe me —"

Trebek: "That's the end of regular Jeopardy. Mr. Trump has minus $1,800, Senator Cruz has minus $1,400 and Governor Kasich has the lead with $0."

Kasich (*clicking on his buzzer with frustration*): "I just can't get my buzzer to work to get a word in."

TWENTY-THREE

Caitlin Jenner's Bathroom Controversy
April 2016

Ted Cruz ✓
@tedcruz

Common sense: grown men shouldn't be in bathrooms w/ little girls. @realDonaldTrump told us he could be PC, but wow.

7:49 AM - 21 Apr 2016

566 replies 1,335 retweets 1,467 likes

Ted Cruz ✓
@tedcruz

We shouldn't be facilitating putting little girls alone in a bathroom w/ grown men. That's just a bad, bad, bad idea

7:06 AM - 21 Apr 2016

357 replies 1,144 retweets 1,743 likes

Satirical Press International — According to a spokesperson for Caitlin Jenner, the transgender celebrity was overwhelmed by Donald Trump's kind show of support during a *Today Show* interview this week.

"Caitlin is a devout fan of *The Today Show*," said the spokesperson. "Al Roker in particular. She tuned in the other morning to watch a hard-hitting report on how to make gluten-free whoopee pies and continued for the Trump interview. Caitlin was surprised and overjoyed by Mr. Trump's invitation for her to use any bathroom she wants in Trump Tower. She plans to fly to Manhattan this week to accept the offer."

Upon hearing the news of Ms. Jenner's flight, Mr. Trump said, "We'll be ready for her touchdown."

Trump's invitation may have delighted Ms. Jenner, but it created a backlash from social conservatives. Senator Ted Cruz immediately made denial of LGBT bathroom access a touchstone for his campaign, saying it had to be done "to protect my two young daughters." At the state level, North Carolina and Mississippi passed laws to limit bathroom usage to a person's born gender.

In North Carolina, enforcement of the new law has created a host of unforeseen problems, however. A woman named Denise was denied access to the ladies' room in a small town outside Raleigh: "I have very short hair, never use make up and wear a leather bomber jacket, so this big dude guarding the women's room said I couldn't enter without proof of my birth gender. Look, I don't happen to carry my birth certificate with me, do you? and to be honest, I had to go really bad."

Asked how she resolved the issue, she said, "I had no choice but go to the men's room. What a shit sty! No wonder so many want to use the ladies' room."

In Mississippi, a transgender woman in her twenties from Oxford named Marla was asked why she wanted to use the women's room. "Because I've been a woman for several years and get a lot of super creepy looks in the men's room," she said. "Try, like, putting on lipstick in that crowd."

The SPI reporter mentioned that Senator Cruz said people like Marla wanted access to women's rooms to be with girls like his two daughters. "Is that your motivation?" the reporter asked.

"Heck no! My motivation? If there's a chance Senator Cruz would be in the men's room, I wouldn't go in there in a million years."

Facebook Comments to Article:

██████████████ He should be ashamed of himself. He has daughter's . . .

Like · Reply · Message · April 30, 2016 at 7:33am

██████████████████ Why can't you use a unisex one

Like · Reply · Message · April 30, 2016 at 7:35am

████████████ I'm confused!!!! Lolololo

Like · Reply · Message · April 30, 2016 at 7:54am

████████████ I would like to see it get high velocity lead poisioning

Like · Reply · Message · April 30, 2016 at 8:06am

████████████ Too bad!

Like · Reply · Message · April 30, 2016 at 8:13am

████████████ He should use the men restroom. Still waiting for Kanye West to start wearing a dress. The Kardashians for some reason you seem to do that to people.

Like · Reply · Message · April 30, 2016 at 8:29am

██████████ What a peice of work

Like · Reply · Message · April 12, 2016 at 9:35am

████████████ Too bad...you are the one that screwed up..sorry, no sympathy!

Like · Reply · Message · April 30, 2016 at 11:00am

TWENTY-FOUR

Making America Great Again, One Lawsuit at a Time
May 2016

Satirical Press International — It's noon on CNN, and the beautiful, bespectacled Ashleigh Banfield opens her show, Legal View, with a breaking story:

"In a story with far-reaching implications for the legal and business worlds, we have just learned that Starbucks has been sued by a Chicago woman for putting too much ice in her 24-ounce iced coffee. In addition, the Chicago law firm representing her is turning the dispute into a class action lawsuit. For the details, let's go to Chicago with our own Jake Tapper."

Tapper: "Ashley, I'm standing outside a Starbucks in downtown Chicago with Mary Little, the woman who filed what we're calling the 'Chill' lawsuit against Starbucks for excess ice. Ms. Little, what's this about?"

Little: "I've gone to Starbucks for years for iced coffee. I usually order the 24 ounce version, and after a while, I noticed that there was a lot of ice in the drink."

Tapper: "It's called iced coffee. Do you think it's fair to blame Starbucks for ice?"

Little: "There's too much ice! They say it's 24 ounces, but in reality, it's only about 16 ounces of coffee — the rest is ice. It's false advertising."

Tapper: "So you're suing Starbucks for damages?"

Little: "Yeah, this is America. I have rights."

Tapper: "Did you consider asking for less ice?"

Little: "Why is the burden on customers to have to ask for what is advertised?"

Tapper: "And you expect this to be a class action lawsuit?"

Little: "Yes. There are millions of Americans out there who have been over chilled by Starbucks."

Tapper: "Thanks, Mary. Back to you in New York, Ashleigh."

Banfield: "This just in — the ice controversy is spilling over to McDonald's. For this we go to Dana Bash in Richmond."

Bash: "Ashley, I'm at a McDonald's here in Richmond where a customer, Scottie Belcher, is filing an ice lawsuit against the burger giant today. Mr. Belcher, what's this suit about?"

Belcher (*holding a large McDonald's cup*): "For years, my jumbo Cokes have been gipped by too much ice, so I'm doin' somethin' about it today."

Bash: "You're suing because your sodas have too much ice?"

Belcher: "Not my sodas, Dana, my Cokes. Yes, they got too damn much ice."

Bash: "But aren't your Cokes self-served?"

Belcher: "No, I pour them myself."

Bash: "But don't you determine how much ice goes into your Cokes?"

Belcher: "It's not my fault — they should put warnings on the ice thingy."

Bash: "Warnings?"

Belcher: "Yea, warnings about the truth or consequences of too much ice."

Bash: "I see."

Belcher: "Like the warnings in those Cialis ads on TV, you know with the old guys with hot — "

Bash: "We're out of time. Back to you, Ashley."

Banfield: "After this short break, we will examine a new lawsuit by a high school junior against his parents for his low SAT scores."

Facebook Comments to Article:

██████████ Next thing you know, they will be suing for too much coffee in their coffee! Thanks for the laugh! Loved the satirical reporting.

Like · Reply · Message · May 6, 2016 at 2:09pm

████████████████ Throw it out & we need to make plaintiffs foot the bills for these stupid lawsuits.

Like · Reply · Message · May 6, 2016 at 4:42pm

██████████ These are the same people that paid $2.50 for a bottle of water

Like · Reply · Message · May 6, 2016 at 5:08pm

████████ THIS IS SO STUPID!!!!! ANOTHER WAY FOR SOMEONE TO GET RICH OVER BITCHING ABOUT SOMETHING STUPID!!!!!

Like · Reply · Message · May 6, 2016 at 5:12pm

████████████ People are sue crazy but pull into a McDonald's and see the response when you order a large soda with NO ice!!! Big no no.....it means the are giving you more product and no ice. Buy a large drink sometime with ice pour out the soda and see how little you actually get

Like · Reply · Message · May 6, 2016 at 5:55pm

████████████ But at McDonald's you pour your own soda if you go inside....

Like · Reply · Message · May 6, 2016 at 10:26pm

TWENTY-FIVE

Trump Proposes Bankruptcy Workout for U.S.
May 2016

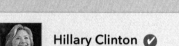
Hillary Clinton ✔
@HillaryClinton

We can't let Trump bankrupt America the way he did his casinos. We need a new chapter in the American Dream – and it can't be Chapter 11.

12:12 PM - 22 Jun 2016
833 replies 1,779 retweets 5,050 likes

Donald J. Trump ✔
@realDonaldTrump

Stop saying I went bankrupt. I never went bankrupt but like many great business people have used the laws to corporate advantage – smart!

9:30 AM - 19 Jun 2015

678 replies 926 retweets 1,154 likes

Satirical Press International — Presumptive Republican Presidential Nominee Donald J. Trump stunned the financial world in an interview on CNBC Thursday. When asked by Jim Cramer of Mad Money if the U.S. should repay its debts in full or create a workout payment system, Trump said, "I would borrow, knowing that if the economy crashed, you could make a deal, an incredible deal — which is what I do, by the way. And if the economy was good, it was good. So, therefore, you can't lose."

Pressed on this answer, the real estate billionaire said, "I've used this approach with four casino bankruptcies — it's a tried and true method, believe me, and it's all about negotiation, folks, and I'm a great negotiator — you won't see me making bad deals, like the nuclear deal with Iran, believe me, I make great deals, really great deals, and I'll make our creditors take 80 cents on the dollar — we've been weak too long, thanks to bad deals."

Cramer responded: "U.S. Treasuries are renewed constantly, and the interest rate is a major determinant of stock and bond values worldwide, as well as mortgage rates, so if creditors thought they're money wasn't safe in the U.S., they'd demand higher rates. Each one percent increase in treasury rates would cost the U.S. almost $200 billion annually."

"Only if we paid it," Trump countered.

"But wouldn't a default significantly reduce our ability to borrow trillions?" Cramer asked.

"I'm not going to reveal my negotiating strategy to the world like Obama — the worst president ever — did with Syria, but we'd find the money elsewhere, believe me, and at lower rates."

"Where? Like Mars?"

"That's not a very nice comment, Jim, but if you must know, we'd get Mexico to pay for it."

"How?" Cramer asked.

"Do you know that Corona is the top selling imported beer in the U.S.?"

"Really?"

"It's because of all the illegals, millions of them, rapists and murderers like Corona, believe me, those are the people taking all the good jobs in America, folks, not that I don't like Hispanics — I posed with a giant taco in my office last week on Cinco De Mayo."

"So what does Corona have to do with our debt?" Cramer asked.

"We'd put a 20% tariff on Corona unless Mexico paid our interest."

"Do you think Congress would back you on that?"

"As long as we don't tax their phoofy craft beers, like Sierra Nevada, or California cabernets, they'll do what I say, believe me. They're a bunch of losers, folks like Little Marco and Lyin' Ted."

"You've already beaten Rubio and Cruz; you don't need to mock them anymore."

Donald J. Trump ✔
@realDonaldTrump

Haters and losers say I wear a wig (I don't), say I went bankrupt (I didn't), say I'm worth $3.9 billion (much more). They know the truth!

2:02 PM - 5 Apr 2014

392 replies   1,033 retweets   1,152 likes

TWENTY-SIX

Conservatives Strike: Ivy League Hires First Republican Professor

May 2016

Satirical Press International — Cambridge, Massachusetts. Amidst the media feeding frenzy over the emerging general election battle between Donald Trump and Hillary Clinton, a story has broken with stunning implications: a university within the Ivy League has hired the first Republican professor in the elite conference's storied history. The identities of the hiring institution and the new professor are being kept secret, however, to avoid campus upheaval and violence.

Mason T. Wallingford IV, spokesperson for the Ivy League, announced the hire in a surprise press conference in Cambridge over the weekend: "For years, our member institutions have sought greater diversity among their faculty and student bodies. We thought, what the heck? — let's try something none of us has done before and experiment with diversity of political views."

Asked why the school and professor have not been identified, Mr. Wallingford said, "The faculty would not, I'm afraid, embrace this new direction. To be honest, we feared protests and threats to the new hire — no one wants cars burning in the streets. We want to give this radical experiment a chance to succeed."

"Won't the truth eventually come out though?" inquired Jake Tapper of CNN, a Dartmouth graduate.

"Of course, that's a risk we take, but we're counseling the professor to avoid voicing his or her opinion on offensive topics," responded Mr. Wallingford.

"Can you give examples of such topics?" asked Tapper.

"The usual topics that are forbidden on campus: free trade, criticism of political correctness, the failure of Communism and Ronald Reagan in general."

"Do you really think you can keep this under wraps?" asked Mr. Tapper, "one peep about improving secondary school performance via increased competition, and the gig's up."

"It's a big risk, granted, but we have several wealthy alumni who demand it. They're big donors, and we had to throw them a bone."

"Aren't there safer ways to introduce political diversity?" asked Lester Holt of NBC News.

"The League considered several alternatives, like seminars on free speech, safe zones for students offended by others' opinions, and even commencement speakers like former New York Mayor Michael Bloomberg. But in the end, we decided to just rip the band aid off."

Meanwhile, across the eight Ivy League campuses, speculation is growing as to the school in question.

"It must be Dartmouth," speculated a Harvard sophomore from Manhattan. "It has the fraternity that inspired Animal House, and I hear their cafeteria serves meat and gluten foods."

TWENTY-SEVEN

Liberals Strike Back: Gluten-Free Dog Treats
May 2016

Satirical Press International — At 8:40 a.m. on a beautiful spring Friday morning in New York, The Today Show set is buzzing with excitement. Following Al Roker's weather forecast from outside Studio 3B, Matt Lauer introduces the next segment:

"Today, we explore a rising health trend sweeping America: gluten-free dog treats. To report on the reaction to this groundbreaking health development, we have Savannah Guthrie outside Rockefeller Center. Savannah, what have you got for us today?"

(An outside shot shows the beautiful Guthrie standing outside next to two dogs and their owners with a huge Today Show crowd with signs cheering behind them)

Guthrie: "Matt, Americans everywhere are looking for healthy alternatives. Well, a dog treat company, Tempt'n Tenders™, has introduced a new line of canine health food snacks that are gluten-free and have no artificial sweeteners."

Lauer: "That's interesting, Savannah. What do the dogs think?"

Guthrie: "I'm are here with a Chihuahua named Flora and her owner,

Betty, from San Diego, and a Black Lab mix named Scat and his owner, Floyd, from Aiken, South Carolina. Let's start with you, Betty. What do you think of this new gluten-free option?"

Betty: "It's wonderful, Savannah — can I give a big shout out to my cousins in San Diego?"

Guthrie: "Go right ahead."

Betty: "Hey, Barb, hey Mike. Go Chargers!"

Guthrie: "I'm sure they loved it. What about these treats?"

Betty: "It's just so great that corporate America is no longer taking advantage of dogs with industrial food and the well-known toxin, gluten, and has produced something dogs would find in their natural state."

Guthrie: "So the new Tempt'n Tenders™ are more what Flora would have eaten roaming the plains thousands of years ago?"

Betty: "Exactly."

(*Floyd interrupts*) **Floyd:** "Except there ain't no Chihuahuas in nature, Betty. I'm 'fraid Flora woulda gotten eaten by a saber tooth cat, Brontosaurus Rex or some such."

(*Betty looks stunned, Guthrie tries not to laugh*)

Guthrie: "So, Floyd, I take it you and Scat are not fans of Tempt'n Tenders™?"

Floyd: "Scat likes 'em just fine, but then again, he eats fresh cat shit right out of the litter box, sprinkled with litter like sesame seeds. Hell, I've seen 'im eat a carp that'd been dead for a week, bones 'n all. Gluten sure ain't gonna kill 'em."

(*Camera inside Studio 3B shows Lauer and Willie Geist in tears laughing*)

Guthrie: "That's an interesting point of view, Floyd. Betty, do you have any closing thoughts?"

Betty: "Well, Floyd here should treat his poor Scat more tenderly."

Floyd: "Ain't nothing wrong with my Scat, and there ain't nothing tender 'bout the mutt, Betty….. But hey look, he's makin' a move on little ol' Flora." *(Before cutting away, camera briefly shows Scat mounting Flora.)*

Facebook Comments to Article:

██████████ If you have Celiac, it's a necessity not a fad. It's nice to not get sick when your dig licks you

Like · Reply · Message · May 28, 2016 at 12:28pm

TWENTY-EIGHT

What Politicians, NRA Leaders & Plaintiffs' Lawyers Have in Common
June 2016

Satirical Press International — Carol Costello of CNN opens her 9:00 a.m. show with a stunning announcement:

Costello: "Scientists at MIT announced today that after a decade-long effort, they have identified the human gene responsible for shameless behavior. Joining me today is Dr. Claus Krefeld. Good morning, doctor."

Krefeld: "Good morning, Carol, thanks for having me."

Costello: "This sounds like a major discovery. Can you explain your findings?"

Krefeld: "For many years, we've collected human DNA data from thousands of individuals in the United States, which was the easy part. The tough part was matching DNA with behavior."

Costello: "What did you find?"

Krefeld: "We found that individuals displaying shameless behavior shared a gene that others didn't have."

Costello: "Who has this gene? What kind of people?"

Krefeld: "I won't name individuals, but the highest concentration of the shameless gene was found in politicians."

Costello: "Thanks, Dr. Obvious. Just look at the current presidential campaign. Who else?"

Krefeld: "NRA executives were only slightly behind politicians in concentration of the shameless gene but within the statistical margin of error."

Costello: "Did you find anything that wasn't obvious?"

Krefeld: "The third highest prevalence of the gene was among plaintiffs' lawyers, like the lawyers suing McDonald's for discriminating against blind people by only having drive thru service at night."

Costello: "For more on this, let's go to our national correspondent, Pamela Brown, reporting live from San Antonio. Good morning, Pamela."

Brown: "Carol, I'm here with Billy Wellers, who is visually impaired, and his attorney, Ricky Jackson, who filed suit yesterday against McDonald's for violating the Americans with Disabilities Act by only serving via drive thru after midnight. Mr. Wellers, what can you say about this?"

Wellers: "Like everyone else, I love Quarter Pounders with cheese, fries and shakes at 2 a.m. after listening to all the late night shows on TV and poundin' a few beers. But I can't even get them because I can't access the drive thru."

Brown: "Because you're visually impaired?"

Wellers: "That's right. Even though I can buy a semi automatic rifle, I can't get a driver's license here in Texas."

Brown: "Have you considered having someone else drive you, especially since you were pounding beers?"

Wellers: "Yes, ma'am. I tried a taxi driver, but it didn't work."

Brown: "Because of the late hour?"

Wellers: "No, because I couldn't find one who spoke English."

Brown: "Thanks, Mr. Wellers. Back to you in New York, Carol."

TWENTY-NINE

Democrats, Republicans Spar Over Tree Pollen

June 2016

Satirical Press International — CNN's bespectacled morning anchor, Carol Costello, opens her show at 9 a.m. with the following announcement:

Costello: "As the allergy season erupts all over America, the culture wars between right and left have shifted to a surprising new area: tree pollen. Yards, cars and streets have been covered in pollen. What is usually a nightmare for allergy sufferers has turned into a political lightning rod as political parties craft their respective platforms. To discuss this further, I'd like to welcome our guests on this topic, former Senator and Presidential candidate Rick Santorum and California Senator Barbara Boxer. Welcome."

Santorum and Boxer: "Good morning."

Costello: "Let's start with you Senator Santorum. What's the issue here with tree pollen?"

Santorum: "Tree pollen is everywhere, and our society — with its deteriorating values — has just accepted it. Do you all know what pollen is? It's trees out shamelessly looking for mates. We've got to nip this immorality in the bud!"

Costello: "Senator Boxer, the Democratic Party has been at the forefront of social change in the culture wars, but have trees gone too far?"

Boxer: "Trees have been under attack for centuries — clear cutting, deforestation, Lincoln Logs, etc. Now social conservatives are calling pollen immoral. This isn't 1950, Carol. Trees have a right to a social life."

Santorum: "It's not fair for trees to impose their loose values on the rest of us! Their actions are seen uncensored everyday by children of all ages across America."

Boxer: "It's no worse than the lyrics in most rap songs, Carol."

Santorum: "I have to disagree with you, Senator. Think about it. Trees are reaching out indiscriminately and mating right and left — it's unnatural."

Boxer: "Unnatural?"

Santorum: "Absolutely. Do you know that trees often mate with themselves? It's a sick form of tree hugging, wouldn't you say? Cam and Mitchell of Modern Family don't even condone that kind of thing."

Boxer: "I'm sure if you asked Cameron and Mitchell, they would say it's fine."

Costello: "Senator Boxer, what about the millions of Americans who suffer from tree pollen allergies, like me?"

Boxer: "I don't understand how that's relevant to the morality of trees."

Costello: "Why should we all suffer just because trees want to hook up?"

Facebook Comments to Article:

████████████ I guess next they will want to start banning the trees.
Like · Reply · Message · June 12, 2016 at 2:28am

████████████ Our government never ceases to amaze me as to what they ban next!! Haven't they got more important things to take care of like jobs, better economy and I could go on and on!!
Like · Reply · Message · June 13, 2016 at 6:02pm

████████████ ?

Like · Reply · Message · June 14, 2016 at 12:52am

THIRTY

Trump's Brilliant Legal Strategy
June 2016

Donald J. Trump ✔
@realDonaldTrump

I hope the Mexican judge is more honest than the Mexican businessmen who used the court system to avoid paying me the money they owe me.

2:51 PM - 5 Mar 2015

442 replies   1,372 retweets   893 likes

Donald J. Trump ✔
@realDonaldTrump

I have a judge in the Trump University civil case, Gonzalo Curiel (San Diego), who is very unfair. An Obama pick. Totally biased-hates Trump

2:45 PM - 30 May 2016

2,744 replies   3,787 retweets   13,227 likes

Satirical Press International — CNN's bespectacled legal expert, Ashleigh Banfield, on Legal View:

Banfield: "The legal world is in a tizzy this week over putative Republican candidate Donald Trump's assertion that Federal Judge Gonzalo Curiel is biased against Trump in the Trump University fraud case because he's Mexican. To discuss this, we have the candidate himself live from San Diego, California. Good morning to you, Mr. Trump."

Trump (*with his characteristic tough frown*): "Hello, Ashley."

Banfield: "Mr. Trump, why do you say that Judge Curiel is biased against you?"

Trump: "Because he's a Mexican — which I'm not saying is bad, but we're going to build a wall not far from here, believe me, a big wall. It'll make the Great Wall of China look like a picket fence, folks, trust me."

Banfield: "But Judge Curiel was born in Indiana and went to college and law school at Indiana University."

Trump: "You can take the judge out of Mexico but not the Mexico out of the judge. I hear he drinks Corona Beer and eats en-she-la-ta-tas every day. He's as Mexican as Montezuma's Revenge and just as upsetting, trust me. I know laws and the legal world—there's probably no one else in the world who knows more about laws than I do, believe me, I have a big brain."

Banfield: "So, Mr. Trump, does this mean any judge whose race, religion or gender has been mocked or criticized by you is not fit to preside over any Trump legal case?"

Trump: "Absolutely, having biased media like the sleazes at ABC News is bad enough, but biased judges are intolerable, and I won't stand for it."

Banfield: "Mr. Trump, you and your organizations have thousands of lawsuits filed against you every year, correct?"

Trump: "All by a bunch of losers like Hillary Clinton, Crooked Hillary I call her. Worst Secretary of State ever — no stamina, trust me."

Banfield: "So by denouncing Mexicans, Muslims, the Pope, women, the disabled and others, you would theoretically shrink the pool of potential judges for your cases to white males with no college education."

Trump: "Don't forget short people, like Little Marco."

Banfield: "My apologies. So all that would be left to preside over your cases would be white males with no college education who aren't short?"

Trump: "That's correct."

Banfield: "No judges fit those criteria. Every judge would have to recuse him or herself from your cases……. Every case against you would have to be — oh, now I get it."

Hillary Clinton ✓
@HillaryClinton

@realdonaldtrump's bigoted comments about a Latino judge are so disgusting, even other Republicans are offended.

5:04 AM - 6 Jun 2016

1,658 replies 6,572 retweets 10,267 likes

Hillary Clinton ✓
@HillaryClinton

Trump called Latinos "bad hombres" on Wednesday. It's not even the most insulting thing he said about the community.

10:15 AM - 21 Oct 2016

1,180 replies 1,587 retweets 4,327 likes

Donald J. Trump ✓
@realDonaldTrump

I should have easily won the Trump University case on summary judgement but have a judge, Gonzalo Curiel, who is totally biased against me.

2:55 PM - 30 May 2016

4,434 replies 4,030 retweets 14,569 likes

 Donald J. Trump ✓
@realDonaldTrump

Happy #CincoDeMayo! The best taco bowls are made in Trump Tower Grill. I love Hispanics!

11:57 AM - 5 May 2016

22,534 replies 84,942 retweets 119,539 likes

Facebook Comments to Article:

██████████ Exactly

Like · Reply · Message · June 10, 2016 at 12:40pm

██████████ That is not what Trump..wants...at all..

Like · Reply · Message · June 12, 2016 at 12:02am

██████████ From what I heard today, a plaintiff in one of the cases wanted off the case when a tape of her came out, praising the course. The judge allowed the case to go forward WITH NO FRIGGIN' PLAINTIFF. That's B.S.

Like · Reply · Message · June 12, 2016 at 12:47am

██████████ Trump is wrong, and he can get an impartial trial with a judge of any racial political persuasion, why'd we supposedly have to have this on the Supreme Court? A big deal was made about having the perspective of a Latino woman on the bench, as she ar...See More

Liberal Supreme Court Justice Agrees with Donald Trump in Judge Flap! - Eagle…

EAGLERISING.COM

Like · Reply · Message · June 12, 2016 at 6:07am

███████████ Why do you go to such links to say things that make you look stupid. You know trump did not say these things that's your words not his

Like · Reply · Message · June 12, 2016 at 7:45am

William Goodspeed Phyllis, yes, he did not say those things (except criticizing Judge Curiel). It's satire only, meant to entertain, sometimes with a message.

Like · Reply · Message · June 12, 2016 at 9:15am

███████████ Wipe the drool off of your chin fool.

Like · Reply · Message · June 12, 2016 at 10:02am

███████████ Vote Trump

Like · Reply · Message · June 12, 2016 at 12:00pm

███████████ You can't say much about intelligence, if you vote democrat

Like · Reply · Message · June 12, 2016 at 3:50pm

███████████ Judge Curiel's string ties with CA. La Raza, "The Race" lawyers association.. La Raza and their racial supremacist concepts (denounced by chavez) really disqualify this judge.

Like · Reply · Message · June 12, 2016 at 10:55pm

███████████ Sounds good that gets rid of the liberals and put common sense back on the bench. Down with college education can't balance a checkbook move back home because there are no jobs. Get real people!

Like · Reply · Message · June 13, 2016 at 12:56am

████████ I dont care much for Trump, and even less gor Hilary, but I had no idea that the Pope might end up as judge if I am ever in a court case. Eye roll.

Like · Reply · Message · June 13, 2016 at 3:10am

████████ How about a judge that doesn't belong to a racial hate group. Is not the anker baby to an illegal alien. And isn't participating in a boycott of all things Trump? This man needs to recuse himself according to the law!

Like · Reply · Message · June 13, 2016 at 10:00am

████████ Well this post takes the cake as the dumbest one I have seen on Facebook. And I have seen a lot of dumb ones. It takes little brain power to shred the assumptions required to make this idiotic statement.

Like · Reply · Message · June 13, 2016 at 10:19a.m.

████████ A fools interpretation of someone's motives not knowing his heart

Like · Reply · Message · June 13, 2016 at 11:13am

████████ Do you really think he'll get a fair trial from a Judge with 2 ties to Mexican HATE GROUPS?

Like · Reply · Message · June 13, 2016 at 4:19pm

*Banned Blogger William Goodspeed
in a Moment of Self-Reflection*

THIRTY-ONE

Trump Trashes Media, Bloggers
June 2016

 Hillary Clinton ✔
@HillaryClinton

Trump has banished members of the press who have criticized him. Is there any doubt he would do the same as president?

10:14 AM - 13 Jul 2016

1,198 replies   1,233 retweets   3,255 likes

Satirical Press International — In CNN's Situation Room, Wolf Blitzer opens his show with a stunning announcement:

Blitzer: "We have some news breaking today about a new controversy surrounding the Trump campaign. On the heels of the campaign revoking the press pass for the Washington Post for biased reporting, Mr. Trump announced today that he is banning the humor blogger, William Goodspeed, from campaign events. To comment on this, we have Mr. Trump live from Charlotte, North Carolina. Mr. Trump, thank you for joining us."

Trump: "Of course. The media are a bunch of liars, all of them, the worst kind. Shameful people, trust me. We're not going to take it any more, folks, believe me. Not going to take it. From now on, Goodspeed

— who is the worst blogger ever — is no longer welcome at our events, no longer welcome. He can wait in the loser lounge with reporters from the Washington Post."

Blitzer: "What has Mr. Goodspeed done to evoke such a response? Has he mischaracterized your campaign or written offensive material? Or does he have a liberal bias? Has he reported on the size of your hands?"

Trump: "All of the above. Total lies. He wrote that I want to disqualify all judges who are not white men. Not true. Just Mexican judges. We're going to build a wall, folks, a big wall, so big you will be able to see it from the space station, believe me. Immigration is killing America. And maybe disqualify Muslim judges too — until we find out what's going on. And women."

Blitzer: "Has he written about the size of your hands?"

Trump: "My staff caught him rifling through my golf bag, trust me."

Blitzer: "Why? Why would Mr. Goodspeed be interested in your golf bag?"

Trump: "He wanted to measure my golf gloves, but I have no trouble with the size of my gloves, believe me. No trouble."

Blitzer: "For a response, let's go to Mr. Goodspeed himself, who is live from Traverse City, Michigan. Good afternoon."

Goodspeed (*standing with Grand Traverse Bay in the background*): "Thanks, Wolf, for having me on the show."

Blitzer: "You just heard Mr. Trump's remarks about you. How do you respond?"

Goodspeed: "I think this is just a case of miscommunication — many Trump supporters read my blog and mistakenly believe I'm making up facts."

Blitzer: "Can you give an example?"

Goodspeed: "Sure. On April 1st, I wrote how aliens had replaced Donald Trump for the past year as a prank and trained the robot to say outrageous things, and how they were bringing back the real Trump with their apologies."

Blitzer: "And you're now saying this wasn't true?"

Goodspeed (*chuckles*): "Yes, breaking news."

Blitzer: "How are readers supposed to know it's not true?"

Goodspeed (*barely containing himself*): "Isn't it obvious?"

Blitzer: "Apparently not. What proof do we have it's not true?"

Goodspeed: "Because he keeps saying outrageous things, even after his body was supposedly returned."

Donald J. Trump ✓
@realDonaldTrump

@FoxNews has been treating me very unfairly & I have therefore decided that I won't be doing any more Fox shows for the foreseeable future.

9:02 AM - 23 Sep 2015

5,417 replies   5,738 retweets   10,264 likes

Donald J. Trump ✓
@realDonaldTrump

Do you ever notice that lightweight @megynkelly constantly goes after me but when I hit back it is totally sexist. She is highly overrated!

7:00 PM - 22 Sep 2015 from Manhattan, NY

1,531 replies   2,730 retweets   6,646 likes

Donald J. Trump ✔
@realDonaldTrump

Just announced that in the history of @CNN, last night's debate was its highest rated ever. Will they send me flowers & a thank you note?

10:17 AM - 17 Sep 2015

1,572 replies   4,998 retweets   10,430 likes

POST-INAUGURATION POST SCRIPT:

The Trump relationship with the media did not improve after the election and inauguration:

Donald J. Trump ✔
@realDonaldTrump

The FAKE NEWS media (failing @nytimes, @NBCNews, @ABC, @CBS, @CNN) is not my enemy, it is the enemy of the American People!

1:48 PM - 17 Feb 2017

79,160 replies   51,192 retweets   162,671 likes

Donald J. Trump ✔
@realDonaldTrump

The Democrats had to come up with a story as to why they lost the election, and so badly (306), so they made up a story - RUSSIA. Fake news!

6:39 AM - 16 Feb 2017

62,438 replies   27,299 retweets   123,225 likes

Donald J. Trump ✔
@realDonaldTrump

The fake news media is going crazy with their conspiracy theories and blind hatred. @MSNBC & @CNN are unwatchable. @foxandfriends is great!

3:40 AM - 15 Feb 2017

38,024 replies   26,252 retweets   106,170 likes

Donald J. Trump ✓
@realDonaldTrump

Any negative polls are fake news, just like the CNN, ABC, NBC polls in the election. Sorry, people want border security and extreme vetting.

4:01 AM - 6 Feb 2017

64,550 replies 36,973 retweets 164,656 likes

Facebook Comments to Article:

████████████ Trump world where the 2nd amendment reigns supreme and the 1st amendment is dead

Like · Reply · Message · June 17, 2016 at 8:36pm

████████████ If the glove don't fit you must acquit ! TRUMP 16 !

Like · Reply · Message · June 18, 2016 at 9:44pm

████████████ I don't know how Donald trump can say that. We all know the media is fair and balanced and always tells the truth. They have no agenda.

Like · Reply · Message · June 19, 2016 at 12:10pm

████████████ I suppose he's the only one (Trump) permitted to practice free speech. Hmmm!!

Like · Reply · Message · June 20, 2016 at 1:15pm

████████████ 2016 Primary Elections, Political Satire

Like · Reply · Message · June 20, 2016 at 1:43pm

THIRTY-TWO

Satirical Press International — Last night, the United States Senate defeated several different gun safety initiatives brought in the wake of the tragic mass Orlando bar shooting. After the fight, Senate Majority Leader Mitch McConnell held a press conference:

McConnell: "Thank you all for coming. Instead of offering any prepared remarks, I will answer questions."

Erin Burnett (CNN): "Senator McConnell, what was it like in there?"

McConnell: "It was a hard fought battle, Erin. As you know, we had to overcome considerable special interests tonight."

Burnett: "You mean the 92% of Americans who favor expanded background checks for gun purchases?"

McConnell: "There's a margin of error in every poll."

Burnett: "But still."

McConnell: "In the end, it was 100 of us against three hundred and twenty million men, women and children. It was like that glorious movie, 300, where a few hundred Spartan soldiers held off the entire

Persian army, who are Iranians, by the way. We're not as buff as those guys, and some of us guys are gals, but we showed some moxie in there."

Joe Scarborough (MSNBC): "Senator McConnell, recent polls show that 85% of Americans and 90% of my fellow Republicans agree that 'no fly list' terrorist suspects should not be allowed to purchase firearms, yet for some unfathomable reason, the Senate would not pass a law forbidding it."

McConnell: "The majority isn't always right, Joe — they elected President Obama, for example."

Scarborough: "But you can't get 85% of Americans to agree the moon landing was real."

McConnell: "Because they don't trust the liberal, pro-science media, like your network and CNN."

Scarborough: "Do you believe the moon landing was real?"

McConnell: "That's not for me to say."

Scarborough: "Is overwhelming public opinion relevant to the Senate?"

McConnell: "Not when it comes to the Second Amendment. Our Founding Fathers could not have envisioned a prohibition based on a no fly list."

Lester Holt (NBC): "So you're saying suspected terrorists have Second Amendment rights?"

McConnell: "Guns don't kill, people do. The problem is our laws are too soft on terrorists."

Holt: "What do you mean?"

McConnell: "We need more deterrence against terrorist attacks and mass shootings by bringing back the death penalty."

Holt: "But almost all these perpetrators martyr themselves or commit suicide."

McConnell: "That's not all bad — it saves considerable taxpayer money wasted on endless appeals by liberal defense lawyers. These are bad people."

Holt: "Liberal defense lawyers?"

McConnell: "Just one small step above terrorists. We need to throw them all in jail without a trial."

Holt: "Are you aware of other Amendments to the Constitution?"

McConnell: "Well, there must be at least one other since we have the Second Amendment, but none come to mind. Let me get back to you on that."

Hillary Clinton ✔
@HillaryClinton

Background checks and an assault weapons ban might not stop every attack–but they'll stop some, and save lives. We need to fight for them.

10:29 AM - 13 Jun 2016

922 replies   3,676 retweets   9,740 likes

Donald J. Trump ✔
@realDonaldTrump

Crooked Hillary wants to get rid of all guns and yet she is surrounded by bodyguards who are fully armed. No more guns to protect Hillary!

5:49 AM - 21 May 2016

4,079 replies   15,701 retweets   40,028 likes

Donald J. Trump ✔
@realDonaldTrump

Crooked Hillary Clinton wants to essentially abolish the 2nd Amendment. No gun owner can ever vote for Clinton!

6:51 PM - 20 May 2016

2,425 replies 8,210 retweets 20,759 likes

Donald J. Trump ✔
@realDonaldTrump

Great day in Kentucky with Wayne LaPierre, Chris Cox & the @NRA! #MakeAmericaGreatAgain #Trump2016

2:55 PM - 20 May 2016

1,223 replies 4,711 retweets 15,207 likes

Donald J. Trump ✔
@realDonaldTrump

Donald J. Trump Retweeted NRA

Thank you! An honor to be the first candidate ever endorsed by the @NRA- prior to @GOPconvention! #Trump2016 #2A

Donald J. Trump added,

The #NRA is proud to endorse @realDonaldTrump #NRAAM

1:06 PM - 20 May 2016

1,413 replies 6,824 retweets 17,032 likes

Facebook Comments to Article:

████████████ This is so wrong

Like · Reply · Message · June 22, 2016 at 11:25pm

█████████████████ You need to resign now you corrupt little bitch

Like · Reply · Message · June 23, 2016 at 12:24am

████████████ It's because their plan fell apart they didn't expect Trump to ruin their little thieving world they have stole millions from us and they are scared if Trump wins he's going to expose all of them

Like · Reply · Message · June 23, 2016 at 12:26am

████████████ Political elites in both parties. Not a dimes worth of difference in any of them. Trump is not a politician. Vote for Trump the only chance for a real change in the Federal government.

Like · Reply · Message · June 23, 2016 at 1:46am

████████████ Mitch isn't that bright to retort like that satire.... besides,he's not that conservative

Like · Reply · Message · June 23, 2016 at 3:41am

████████████ Touché turtle needs to be gone!

Like · Reply · Message · June 23, 2016 at 8:43am

████████████ Them kickbacks and vacations is the bomb...

Like · Reply · Message · June 23, 2016 at 2:15pm

████████████ He's a Pos

Like · Reply · Message · June 23, 2016 at 2:35pm

████████████ 92% in favor you crazy liberals

Like · Reply · Message · June 23, 2016 at 5:13pm

████████████ This is fake

Like · Reply · Message · June 23, 2016 at 6:09pm

████████████ 92% don't want due process? just willing to give up their guns? bullshit!

Like · Reply · Message · June 23, 2016 at 6:44pm

████████████ Bullshit

Like · Reply · Message · June 23, 2016 at 8:33pm

████████████ It's satire. Nez pas?

Like · Reply · Message · June 23, 2016 at 9:33pm

Facebook Comments to Proposal by Author for Universal Background Checks After Orlando Massacre:

████████████ Trump is right, we have weak leaders who are too worried about being politically correct. If the GOP leadership won't say the words "Radical rightwing gun nuts," they will never solve the problem. The NRA and the rightwing agenda are slathering the Con...*See More*

Like · Reply · Message · June 14, 2016 at 8:11am

████████████ well said.

Like · Reply · Message · June 14, 2016 at 12:02pm

████████████ I've been sitting here thinking about how to respond to this for some time now. I hope your modest proposal is shared and a dialogue is begun; but I don't think many NRA supporters, who might happen to read this, will be in favor of universal regulati...*See More*

Like · Reply · Message · June 14, 2016 at 1:46pm

████████████ There is a ban on assault weapons and military grade weapons. Where've you been?

Like · Reply · Message · June 14, 2016 at 1:46pm

█████████ The ban on assault and military grade weapons expired in 2013. So we know where you have been.

Like · Reply · Message · June 14, 2016 at 2:56pm

████████████ Assault weapons refers to fully automatic firearms and they've been banned. If you're referring to semi-automatic firearms now that's a different question. If you don't know the difference, well...,

Like · Reply · Message · June 14, 2016 at 2:58pm

████████████ I don't know the difference. I just did the research on the law and semi-automatic firearms were included and defined as assault weapons in the original law.

Read all about it http://www.criminaldefenselawyer.com/.../
the-federal...

Like · Reply · Message · June 14, 2016 at 3:22pm

▓▓▓▓▓▓▓ Suffice to say even the article mentions it's
difficult because the term assault weapon does not have a
single definition so I can see where we lost each other. When
I hear "military grade assault weapon" I refer it to the M16
which is the full auto mi...*See More*

Like · Reply · Message · June 14, 2016 at 3:45pm

▓▓▓▓▓▓▓ Watching all these posts on banning firearms.:
Interesting..Wasn't the purpose of second amendment and
constitution to "Limit" power and encroachment of federal
government? Limiting controlling access more and more to
firearms was huge concern. "A wel...*See More*

Like · Reply · Message · June 14, 2016 at 11:25pm

▓▓▓▓▓▓▓ My point being it's in the heart of humankind.
And so one of the results of living and valuing an open,
liberal, and free society is that we also invite the practice of
evil. No bans on this or that will protect us from the intent of
evil. It will find its way, because it is in the heart of humans.
Any real doubt on the concept of original sin?

Like · Reply · Message · June 15, 2016 at 2:31pm

▓▓▓▓▓▓▓ Fair 'nuff, Hitch....but at least when we permit people
to drive a car we make them register it, get trained on how to use
it and get a license. Won't stop him from using it as a weapon, but
We allow people to buy very dangerous guns - tools that wer...
See More

Like · Reply · Message · June 15, 2016 at 4:50pm

▓▓▓▓▓▓▓ Damn. And I went and shaved. Head, back, legs, the
whole works. Hey, 90 shooting deaths is a slow month here in
Chicago. Our forefathers did not foresee automatic weapons

and gang-bangers shooting everyone in the neighborhood. Something has got to change.

Like · Reply · Message · June 14, 2016 at 12:00am

███████████ but a ban on assault weapons might reduce the carnage from 100 people to 10, wouldn't that be worth a try

Like · Reply · Message · June 14, 2016 at 7:57am

███████████ If we can drive without a license, we should be able to have a gun without a license. Oh, wait...

Like · Reply · Message · June 14, 2016 at 12:25pm

███████████ Hey. here's a thought. How about not selling assault weapons to guys who have been on the FBI watch list since 2013.

Like · Reply · Message · June 14, 2016 at 6:51pm

███████████ My humble suggestion is for those who wish to purchase an assault rifle undergo a mental health evaluation and be required to present proof of being cleared by a psychologist at the time of purchase. We have far greater restrictions on Class II narcotics, like oxycodone, which, unlike assault rifles, only kill one person at a time.

Like · Reply · Message · June 14, 2016 at 6:55pm

███████████ We do background checks for things like real estate licensing but not for guns and assault rifles.... hmmmmmmm It is beyond my comprehension!

Like · Reply · Message · June 14, 2016 at 7:36pm

███████████ Apparently not one of you understands two basic notions. The first notion No assault rifle is legal in America already. An assault rifle is more powerful than the legal long guns commonly known as Armalite Rifles (AR15). AR guns do not shoot in autom...See More

Like · Reply · Message · June 14, 2016 at 9:39pm

███████████ The second notion - most hunters and patriots

who oppose gun restrictions do so for one primary reason. The one reason is that an armed populace is a discouragement to a political entity intent on disenfranchising a civilian population for the politic...See More

Like · Reply · Message · June 14, 2016 at 9:58pm

████████████ I hope not, semiauto rifles are no more to blame than semi auto handguns. The best defense against crazed religiuos jihadis is an armed populace and a government that enforces existing laws very strictly. No way that perp should have had weapons, no way.

Like · Reply · Message · June 14, 2016 at 11:04pm

████████████ If the best defense is an armed populace then where is this populace when these mass killings happen, Gordon? Where are YOU & your guns when these crimes happen?

Like · Reply · Message · June 15, 2016 at 2:45am

████████████ Thought - extensive credit checks to buy a house, car, etc. Why not extensive background checks to buy a gun? Just does not make sense. But have no fear Gordon , if our government did not have the courage, the strength of character to pass serious gun laws after 20 children were killed in Newtown, they never will.

Like · Reply · Message · June 15, 2016 at 6:28am

████████████ I am deeply saddened when we lose so many young defenseless adults. How I wish just one of those kids had a weapon on them to do the sick beast in.

Like · Reply · Message · June 15, 2016 at 6:40am

THIRTY-THREE

Americans, Trump Cheer Brexit
June 2016

Donald J. Trump ✔
@realDonaldTrump

Many people are equating BREXIT, and what is going on in Great Britain, with what is happening in the U.S. People want their country back!

2:43 PM - 24 Jun 2016

3,974 replies   9,921 retweets   28,159 likes

Satirical Press International — In a nationwide referendum, the people of the United Kingdom voted to leave the European Union, shocking the world. To understand how Americans view this monumental change, Satirical Press International sent its reporter, David Snidely, to the Santa Monica Pier to interview young beach goers. Snidely approaches four young people in their 20s, three girls with trim figures in bikinis, and a young man with a bathing suit below his knees and a baseball hat on backwards.

Snidely (*to the group*): "Hi, I'm David Snidely from SPI and was wondering if I could ask you a few questions about the British situation?"

First girl, a stunning blonde (*giggling*): "Okay."

Boy: "Cool, bro."

Snidely (*to the first girl*): "Were you surprised about the British independence vote?"

First girl: "I'm, like, totally shocked. Didn't we, like, go independent from Britain about 150 years ago after the Gettysburg Address?"

Second Girl, *a beautiful brunette wearing aviator glasses:* "Oh yeah, I remember that from junior year in high school — go Bears!"

Snidely: "The Gettysburg Address?"

Second Girl: "Yeah, like. 'Four score and some years ago,

> *Our fathers, suffering from incontinence,*
>
> *Started a new nation,*
>
> *Conceived with liberties*
>
> *And justice for all.'*"

Snidely: "That's impressive."

Second Girl: "Thanks. I had to memorize it for, like, my history class. As an American, it really gets me every time I hear it."

Snidely: "It really got me too, to be honest."

Snidely (*to the third girl*): "What do you think about the British separation?"

Third Girl, *a blonde with visibly tight abdominal muscles:* "I'm not surprised really — because of the tea issue."

Snidely: "What tea issue?"

Third Girl: "You know, throwing the tea in New York Harbor."

Snidely: "But that was more than —"

Third Girl: "Americans shouldn't drink English tea anymore — it's not healthy, especially with milk and sugar. We should all drink green tea. It's full of antioxidants and is gluten free."

Snidely: "That's interesting."

Third Girl: "I'm kind of a health nut. Are you wearing sunscreen, Mr. Snidely? I've got some organic sunscreen tucked in the back of my bathing suit…"

Snidely: "No, that's okay, thanks."

Third Girl: "So if we all switch to green tea, we don't need the British. Oh, and we shouldn't drink pasteurized cow milk anyway."

Snidely (*to the young man*): "Do you agree with your friends here?"

Boy: "Yeah, bro, I'm, like, totally stoked about soy milk."

Snidely: "And about the British vote?"

Boy: "Totally. After watching Downton Abbey with my girlfriend, I'm, like, you dudes need to chill."

Donald J. Trump ✔
@realDonaldTrump

The media is unrelenting. They will only go with and report a story in a negative light. I called Brexit (Hillary was wrong), watch November

6:18 AM - 27 Jun 2016

3,770 replies   6,767 retweets   21,499 likes

Donald J. Trump ✔
@realDonaldTrump

They will soon be calling me MR. BREXIT!

5:11 AM - 18 Aug 2016

11,636 replies   17,655 retweets   38,705 likes

Donald J. Trump ✔
@realDonaldTrump

Crooked Hillary Clinton, who called BREXIT 100% wrong (along with Obama), is now spending Wall Street money on an ad on my correct call.

4:33 AM - 26 Jun 2016

2,076 replies   7,435 retweets   21,302 likes

Facebook Comments to Article:

▆▆▆▆▆▆ It's very important to have a solid foundation in our country's history to make such observations!

Like · Reply · Message · June 27, 2016 at 5:26pm

▆▆▆▆▆▆ Like, maybe you should, like, redo elementary.

Like · Reply · Message · June 27, 2016 at 11:51pm

▆▆▆▆▆▆ They're young, pretty and oh so stupid.
One day they'll reproduce.
Wait, this is starting to sound like some punk song.

Like · Reply · Message · June 28, 2016 at 3:50am

▆▆▆▆▆▆ F. The U.N. America should get out now

Like · Reply · Message · June 28, 2016 at 5:32am

▆▆▆▆▆▆ Wow

Like · Reply · Message · June 28, 2016 at 7:58am

▆▆▆▆▆▆ I thought the revolution divided us from England.

Like · Reply · Message · June 28, 2016 at 9:12am

William Goodspeed Thanks for reading my political satire! I hope you enjoy it and will sign up to receive alerts when the new ones come out, usually once or twice per week. P.S. I've actually seen videos of interviews like this.

Like · Reply · Message · June 28, 2016 at 9:57am

Jenny Green Love your work, William Goodspeed! Your satire pieces always make me laugh! They are so outrageous that people actually believe them! Perfection!
Like · Reply · Message · June 28, 2016 at 10:07am

 A new kind of satire. A little funny and a little not. Nevertheless, still satire when we read between the lines.
Like · Reply · Message · June 28, 2016 at 2:38pm

😎
Like · Reply · Message · June 28, 2016 at 6:18pm

It was after the Boer wars!!
Like · Reply · Message · June 28, 2016 at 7:21pm

THIRTY-FOUR

Americans Seek Canadian Mates
June 2016

Satirical Press International — CNN's beautiful morning anchor, Carol Costello, comes on the air after a reverse mortgage advertisement featuring Henry Winkler. Her microphone comes on prematurely....

Costello: "No, I don't know how the hell reverse mortgages work either —"

(*After a brief pause*) **Costello:** "Excuse me. As the American presidential campaign heats up and Donald Trump and Hillary Clinton win their respective parties' nominations, several thousand Americans are looking for love north of the border. A new web site, Maplematch.com, works to link Americans fleeing a Trump or Clinton presidency with willing Canadians. For further details, let's go to Anderson Cooper outside Niagara Falls. Anderson, what are you seeing?"

AC: "Carol, business is booming here along the U.S.-Canadian border. Ever since Trump and Clinton became the presumptive nominees, thousands of Americans have joined Maplematch.com, looking for potential Canadian spouses to shortcut the immigration process."

Costello: "Where are you seeing the biggest impact?"

AC: "Bars and restaurants, for sure, and the hotel business has gotten brisk."

Costello: "Have you seen it happen?"

AC: "Yes, I was at a Tim Horton's and could see people wandering in and scanning the crowd. Usually, they shake hands and sit down with someone, but a few times, I saw them turn briskly away and bolt for the door."

Costello: "False advertising?"

AC: "Big time. I think some are taking PhotoShop liberties with their Maplematch.com profile pictures."

Costello: "Can you tell if Americans are fleeing Trump or Clinton?"

AC: "Interesting question, Carol. For some insight, I've got Jacques Les Petitemains, the owner of a restaurant here. Mr. Les Petitemains, thank you for joining us. What type of American customer do you see most?"

Petitemains: "It depends on the American polls."

AC: "What do you mean?"

Petitemains: "When Clinton leads in the polls, we notice many Trump supporters on dates at our restaurant, some from far away as Alabama."

AC: "How can you tell they are Trump supporters?"

Petitemains: "They have NASCAR tee shirts and order Bud Light Lime or sweet tea."

AC: "Sweet tea?"

Petitemains: "Previously unknown in the Great White North. We had to Google the recipe and buy sacks of sugar to make it."

AC: "What happens when Trump leads in the polls?"

Petitemains: "Everything changes. We have frequent requests for vegan dishes and many, many people asking for gluten-free meals. They also insist on free-range chicken."

AC: "How about drinks? Do you see a change in ordering habits?"

Petitemains: "Yes, sir. Many order craft beers, and the hipsters like Pabst Blue Ribbon — you know, in the big cans?"

AC: "One of my faves."

Petitemains: "And the Latinos look nervous and go for tequila or Corona."

AC: "I can imagine. Anything else?"

Petitemains: "The Clinton supporters seem to really like my name."

AC: "Petitemains? Why?"

Petitemains: "Because it means 'small hands' in French."

POST-INAUGURATION POST SCRIPT:

This article was meant to be fictional satire, but alas, many a truth is said in gest. After Donald Trump was elected President, Maple Match was inundated with people signing up, according to The Economist (January 28, 2017). There is also a new site, TrumpSingles.com, to forge new connections between Trump supporters.

Facebook Comments to Article:

████████████ Tom "Donkey-dick" (████) is taken right now, girls!!
Like · Reply · Message · June 30, 2016 at 11:07pm

████████████ Conservatism

In #DogDickDixie always leads to skinheads getting their mouths washed out with their own blood while they kneel in Dixie Mud...
#GodsOtherPeople¥
Like · Reply · Message · July 1, 2016 at 6:46am

██████████ Both . . . the thought of either is significantly horrific. It's time to start feeding these bad politicians to the guillotines . . .
Like · Reply · Message · July 1, 2016 at 11:48am

████████████ Canada doesn't want your asses. True story. You should consider moving to Mexico if you need to flee politicians
Like · Reply · Message · July 1, 2016 at 12:37pm

████████████ Probley the one thats getting paid off by isis
Like · Reply · Message · July 1, 2016 at 1:58pm

██████████ Pfft if they would leave the country over such pitiful B.S. then I guess they weren't really American to begin with.
Like · Reply · Message · July 1, 2016 at 1:59pm

████████ Well, bye
Like · Reply · Message · July 1, 2016 at 2:35pm

███████████ So many American people are leaving already, they selling the homes, they tell you: I'm moving to a different state, and they out of here, I know some people moving to Australia and western Europe countries, I was shocked when I find out, yup they leaving already !
Like · Reply · Message · July 1, 2016 at 2:37pm

██████████ i heard the Canadians chant 4more years for obama . . . Well them spineless little bitches can have that terrorist asshole.. Free of charge.
Like · Reply · Message · July 1, 2016 at 3:19pm

████████████ Canadians dont want inmigration of U.S. citizens going there.Funny.!!!
Like · Reply · Message · July 1, 2016 at 3:47pm

██████████ Lol
Like · Reply · Message · July 1, 2016 at 10:58pm

THIRTY-FIVE

Bill Clinton, Attorney General Lynch Have Quickie on Plane
July 2016

 Donald J. Trump ✔
@realDonaldTrump

Does anybody really believe that Bill Clinton and the U.S.A.G. talked only about "grandkids" and golf for 37 minutes in plane on tarmac?

2:38 PM - 3 Jul 2016

4,093 replies 7,754 retweets 21,750 likes

Satirical Press International — Former President Bill Clinton shocked the world this week when he met privately with U.S. Attorney General Loretta Lynch in a plane on the tarmac of Phoenix Airport. The meeting took everyone by surprise, including leading Democrats, because Clinton's wife, Hillary, is under criminal investigation by the FBI for her email controversy. Republicans prepared to pounce on the appearance of impropriety.

Always on top of political developments, Satirical Press International's stunning political reporter, Sophie Garibaldi, interviewed the former president shortly after the meeting.

Garibaldi: "Mr. President, did you and the Attorney General discuss the

FBI investigation of your wife?"

Clinton: "Absolutely not. At the beginning of our meeting, we agreed that an indictment of Hillary would devastate the Democratic Party, so this was off limits."

Garibaldi: "You said that?"

Clinton: "Just to be above board."

Garibaldi: "Did the fact that she's the Attorney General and investigating your wife have anything to do with the meeting?"

Clinton: "It was a pure coincidence. I'm sitting in my jet on the tarmac, sipping an espresso, and I look out and see Loretta's jet. So I called her up and said 'your plane or mine?'"

Garibaldi: "Did you ever consider that the meeting would appear improper?"

Clinton: "Not at all, Sophie. Hillary knows I often meet with women alone, and it was daytime, a mitigating circumstance. She's gotten used to these things."

Garibaldi: "No, I mean would it appear like you were trying to influence the investigation against your wife?"

Clinton: "The fact that Loretta Lynch is the boss of the organization investigating Hillary is irrelevant."

Garibaldi: "What did you talk about?"

Clinton: "What do people discuss in private jets? — golf, her favorite French Bordeaux wines, hedge fund performances and the like."

Garibaldi: "Nothing related to your wife?" asked Garibaldi, whose dark wavy hair, brown almond-shaped eyes and athletic build seemed to captivate the former president.

Clinton: "Not a thing — it was just a quickie."

Garibaldi: "A quickie?"

Clinton: "Yes."

Garibaldi: "And you didn't discuss anything else?"

Clinton: "Well, we talked about the economic stagnation of the middle class in America and the soaring wealth of the top tenth of 1%, a really sad story."

Garibaldi: "Did you reach any conclusions?"

Clinton: "No, because we started talking about our jets. Hers has a better catering service — the shrimp cocktail was beyond belief by the way. And her jet has a much longer range than mine. She can fly directly to the French Riviera without refueling. I'm seriously considering an upgrade — just a few more speeches to the Saudis, and I can swing it."

Garibaldi: "What do you think Donald Trump will say about this?"

Clinton (*shaking his finger*): "I do not like that man; I do not like that man at all."

Garibaldi: "Didn't you and Hillary go to his wedding?"

Clinton: "It was his third wedding, so no biggie, and between us (*Clinton whispers*), the new Mrs. Trump is easy on the eyes."

Garibaldi: "What do you think Trump'll say about your private meeting?"

Clinton: "The same things, I'm sure — that his plane is bigger."

Donald J. Trump ✔
@realDonaldTrump

Crooked Hillary Clinton knew that her husband wanted to meet with the U.S.A.G. to work out a deal. The system is totally rigged & corrupt!

1:20 PM - 3 Jul 2016

2,740 replies 8,616 retweets 23,948 likes

Facebook Comments to Article:

▌▌▌▌▌▌▌ 30 mins. Is a quickie?
Like · Reply · Message · July 7, 2016 at 10:44pm

▌▌▌▌▌▌▌ TYPICAL BILL CLINTON.
Like · Reply · Message · July 8, 2016 at 11:58am

Kathy Estrada Fisher Just so you know, this isn't true. It's satire.
Like · Reply · Message · July 8, 2016 at 12:19pm

THIRTY-SIX

Déjà vu All Over Again: Melania Trump Speech
July 2016

Satirical Press International — The set of CNN's Situation Room is abuzz the day after beautiful Melania Trump's stirring speech at the Republican National Convention. Wolf Blitzer comes on the air with sensational breaking news:

Blitzer: "From the Situation Room, this is Wolf Blitzer with breaking news about the Melania Trump speech last night at the Republican Convention in Cleveland. According to the New York Times, several passages from Mrs. Trump's speech were nearly identical to the speech given by Michelle Obama at the 2008 Democratic National Convention. To dig deeper into this, we have a speechwriter from the Trump Campaign. Good afternoon, sir."

Speech Writer (whose image is intentionally blurred and voice mechanically altered): "Good afternoon, Wolf."

Blitzer: "We are keeping your identity confidential for your safety and benefit, but for purposes of this interview, can I call you Bobby?"

Speech Writer: "I've always wanted to be called Wayne."

Blitzer: "Okay, Wayne. People say your speech for Mrs. Trump was basically a cut and paste job from Mrs. Obama's speech in 2008. What do you say to this?"

Wayne: "Mrs. Obama stole her speech from the Trumps."

Blitzer: "But her speech was 8 years before Mrs. Trump's. How is that possible?"

Wayne: "The Clintons attended the Trump wedding with Melania, where Mr. Trump outlined his ideas for America in a toast to the bride. They must have recorded it and given it to the Obamas."

Blitzer: "Most Americans would find that hard to believe. Isn't there another explanation, Wayne?"

Wayne: "Mrs. Trump didn't copy anyone, but spoke about truths to be self-evident, among these are life, liberty and the pursuit of happiness."

Blitzer: "You just plagiarized the Declaration of Independence."

Wayne: "No wonder it sounded so familiar."

Blitzer: "Wayne, the language of the speeches is nearly identical in parts. What really happened?"

Wayne: "Umm."

Blitzer: "Wayne, just say it. The American people have a right to know."

Wayne: "I was rusty, okay? I've been Mr. Trump's speechwriter for what, six months now? He's ignored every speech I've written and instead goes on about building a wall and banning Muslims from entering America until we can figure out what's going on. What serious candidate says 'until we can figure out what's going on'? It's embarrassing to me for my friends to think I wrote that stuff."

Blitzer: "This is incredible news. So you're saying that Mr. Trump ignored your speeches?"

Wayne: "It's like being the beer supplier to the Mormon Church, okay? So I just quit writing them."

Blitzer: "Are you saying that Mrs. Trump winged it with her speech too?"

Wayne: "No, her speech was too good. I wasn't expecting to have to write anything for her so me and some buddies had some fun in Cleveland. You know, an Indians game, the Rock 'n Roll Hall of Fame, a downtown pub crawl. After about 3 hours of sleep and several Advil, I found out she needed a speech, and I only had, like, an hour, so I went to work on the internet. It was pretty efficient, though I got distracted looking up old girl friends on Facebook."

Blitzer: "Did you cut and paste the Melania Trump speech?"

Wayne: "Hey, haven't you ever faced a deadline?"

Facebook Comments to Article:

████████████ Be nice to have a little class back in the WH...been a while now.
Like · Reply · Message · July 23, 2016 at 11:12am

████████████ I would be nice if you had some class!!!!
Like · Reply · Message · July 23, 2016 at 5:06pm

████████████████ It could be that it was a copy but than could be she had the same feelings from her heart people are more alike than many like to think we all have pride in our families and hopes and dreams. How many times we used words to that came from those before...*See More*
Like · Reply · Message · July 23, 2016 at 11:46am

████████████ A Trump aid tendered his resignation and admitted he plagiarized Michelle's speech for Malania. I don't know if Trump accepted the resignation or not. I guess the case is closed now.
Like · Reply · Message · July 23, 2016 at 12:20pm

William Goodspeed I don't blame Melania at all. She's great and has a lot of class. It was just some hopefully fun satire.
Like · Reply · Message · July 23, 2016 at 12:23pm

████████████ Peace

Like · Reply · Message · July 23, 2016 at 12:24pm

████████████ As Hillary said about Benghazi.... (foaming at the mouth)..."at this point what difference does it make?

Like · Reply · Message · July 23, 2016 at 4:59pm

███████████ My advice for those who were offended I offer this suggestion. Do not vote for her. (Melania).

Like · Reply · Message · July 23, 2016 at 8:52pm

███████████ Damn Funny !!!

Like · Reply · Message · July 23, 2016 at 11:24pm

████████████ Get over it already.

Like · Reply · Message · July 24, 2016 at 3:02am

███████████ Funny!

Like · Reply · Message · July 24, 2016 at 5:27am

███████████ She would be a much better First Lady than Michelle has been or Bill will be!

Like · Reply · Message · July 24, 2016 at 12:51pm

████████████ Haha-DEMS & DNC IS FALLING APART, THE ROACHES ARE SCATTERING & this is a mute point & silly. TRUMP 2016

Like · Reply · Message · July 24, 2016 at 8:42pm

███████████ Blah blah blah stop already

Like · Reply · Message · July 24, 2016 at 11:07pm

THIRTY-SEVEN

Democratic Convention: White House 'In the Bag'

July 2016

Donald J. Trump ✔
@realDonaldTrump

I always said that Debbie Wasserman Schultz was overrated. The Dems Convention is cracking up and Bernie is exhausted, no energy left!

1:30 PM - 24 Jul 2016

2,354 replies 7,346 retweets 24,517 likes

Donald J. Trump ✔
@realDonaldTrump

The highly neurotic Debbie Wasserman Schultz is angry that, after stealing and cheating her way to a Crooked Hillary victory, she's out!

3:33 PM - 24 Jul 2016

3,175 replies 9,363 retweets 29,799 likes

Satirical Press International — The beautiful, bespectacled Carol Costello opens her morning show from a studio within the Democratic National Convention with a stunning announcement:

Costello: "Good morning, in breaking news, CNN has just learned that Democratic National Committee Debbie Wasserman Schultz has resigned her post as a result of Wikileaks exposing emails from the DNC showing the Committee favored Secretary Hillary Clinton over Senator Bernie Sanders well before the primaries settled the contest. For more on this, let's go to CNN Political Correspondent Pamela Brown on the convention floor."

Brown (*nodding her head while holding a microphone*): "That's right, Carol. Just moments ago, Congresswoman Wasserman Schultz resigned over what many in both parties call an "egregious violation of ethics." The DNC, which is supposed to remain neutral over candidates, clearly showed bias toward Mrs. Clinton. Sanders supporters are furious and have taken their protests to the streets — their beards, dirty blue jeans and tofu takeout causing a stir in Philadelphia."

Costello (*holding her fingers to her right ear piece*): "Hold on a minute, Pamela. We've just learned that Mrs. Clinton has offered a senior position in her campaign to Wasserman Schultz. For more on this, we go to Jake Tapper at Clinton's hotel, where he is joined by Mrs. Clinton herself."

Tapper: "Thank you, Carol. I'm here with the presumptive Democratic nominee, Secretary Hillary Clinton. Mrs. Clinton, can you comment on the Wasserman Schultz hiring?"

Clinton: "Jake, America is a great country, and we need more talented women in senior offices. This is why we thought it critical to hire Debbie Wasserman Schultz."

Tapper: "Hiring women is admirable, Mrs. Clinton, but recent polls suggest that the majority of Americans consider your moral integrity unacceptable, especially after FBI Director Comey's highly critical comments about your emails. In light of this, why hire someone mired in an ethical scandal?"

Clinton: "Because she favored my campaign! I also love her curly hair, which I'm pretty sure is natural."

Tapper: "But don't you worry this will create a more negative impression of your ethics?"

Clinton: "My husband took care of that. After he met privately with the Attorney General, Loretta Lynch, days before the FBI announced it would not indict me, my ethics ratings could only rise. It was brilliant. Plus, I've already started measuring the White House drapes, if you know what I mean (Clinton winks at Tapper)."

Tapper: "Do you find it ironic that Mrs. Wasserman Schultz got in hot water over emails, just like you?"

Clinton: "The Russians and other hackers always pick on great women leaders. It's a badge of honor. And Americans dislike the Russians — no one would ever side with them."

Tapper: "Don't you worry that the Russians or Wikileaks might expose some emails from your private server to tilt the election in favor of Donald Trump?"

Clinton: "Not at all, Jake."

Tapper: Why are you so confident?

Clinton: "I'm pretty sure I deleted all the bad ones, and just in case, I promised Putin the U.S. would not export natural gas to his markets if I'm elected."

Tapper: "And that did it?"

Clinton: "Not quite, he also had to donate $2 million to the Clinton Foundation."

Facebook Comments to Article:

██████████ I think she's just wound too tight!! Kinda like Hillarity's eyeballs and smile!!

Like · Reply · Message · July 28, 2016 at 12:12pm

██████████ Ugly in and out!! Liars, hypocrites!! And FRAUDS!!

Like · Reply · Message · July 28, 2016 at 1:45pm

████████████ ... and her inner hag softens when she smiles!

Like · Reply · Message · July 28, 2016 at 6:38pm

██████████ Hillary and Debbie are both lying rags. I don't give a hoot about their hair. 😫

Like · Reply · Message · July 28, 2016 at 9:39pm

William Goodspeed   The worst

Like · Reply · Message · July 29, 2016 at 8:20pm

THIRTY-EIGHT

Trump Skewers Dem VP Candidate Kaine Over NJ Taxes

July 2016

Donald J. Trump ✓
@realDonaldTrump

Just saw Crooked Hillary and Tim Kaine together. ISIS and our other enemies are drooling. They don't look presidential to me!

1:43 PM - 23 Jul 2016

5,205 replies   9,390 retweets   31,378 likes

Donald J. Trump ✓
@realDonaldTrump

ICYMI: PENCE: I RAN A STATE THAT WORKED; KAINE RAN A STATE THAT FAILED.

7:12 PM - 4 Oct 2016 from Nevada, USA

1,580 replies   8,818 retweets   22,863 likes

Satirical Press International — On the set of The Today Show, Matt Lauer looks into the camera with the beautiful Natalie Morales by his side:

Lauer: Thank you, Natalie, for that provocative segment on making macaroni 'n cheese a sure thing to please fussy kids. Now let's go to a special report from Savannah Guthrie in Fort Collins, Colorado.

185

Savannah Guthrie stands before a crowd of 30 middle-aged women wearing a variety of Fort Collins High School tee shirts and carrying signs.

Guthrie: Thank, Matt. I'm here in sunny Fort Collins with a group celebrating their 25th reunion from Ft. Collins High School. *(Guthrie moves to a group of women in the front).* Hello! Who do we have here?

First Women: My name is Carol Lynn Martin. I'd like to send a big shout out to my wonderful husband and love of my life, Gary! Hi Honey! Go Lambkins!

Group: Good Morning, America! Go Lambkins!!!!!!!!

Guthrie: That's the other show, but no worries. Lambkins?

Carol Lynn: The mascot of Fort Collins High School. Go Lambkins, Rip Them to Pieces!

Guthrie: Baby lambs fight? Anyway, I wanted to ask you about the latest news from Donald Trump. Are you a Trump supporter?

Carol Lynn: Absolutely yes. Make America Great Again! *(huge applause from group).*

Guthrie: Yesterday, Mr. Trump criticized Democratic Vice Presidential Candidate Tim Kaine for raising taxes in New Jersey. What do you say to that *faux pas*?

Carol Lynn: What's a foe paw?

Guthrie: A misstep. It's French.

Carol Lynn: We speak American around here, Savannah *(wild cheers)*, and so should everyone *(even wilder cheers)*!

Guthrie: Okay, but what do you think about Mr. Trump's statement about Tim Kaine?

Carol Lynn: Sorry if it's not politically correct, Savannah, but Mr. Trump says it straight. That's what America needs! (*group cheers wildly*).

Guthrie: But Tim Kaine is a U.S. Senator from Virginia. He has nothing to do with New Jersey or its taxes.

Carol Lynn: The liberal, super-critical media people are always poking at Mr. Trump for what he says.

Guthrie: But what he said is completely untrue.

Carol Lynn: But it's how we feel!!!! (*huge applause*)

Guthrie: You feel angry about higher taxes in New Jersey, even though Mr. Kaine had nothing to do with it and you all live in Colorado?

Carol Lynn: Yes. I heard all about it from Rush Limbaugh on the radio.

Guthrie: There you have it, Matt. The Lambkins are rabid for Donald Trump. Back to you in Studio 3B.

Lauer: Thanks, Savannah. It looks like quite a reunion. Next up: how to keep your dog from rolling in dead fish during your next family picnic.

Facebook Comments to Article:

█████████████ You go Trump!!
Like · Reply · Message · July 29, 2016 at 6:36pm

█████████████ That's all he has, is name calling what a douche bag! Hard to believe people actually voted for this bloviating wind bag! Kinda says a lot about them and their decision making, ability!
Like · Reply · Message · July 29, 2016 at 7:15pm

█████████████ Isn't Kaine indiana?
Like · Reply · Message · July 29, 2016 at 8:54pm

███████████ Kaine is from Virginia Steven Daniel Roche trump screwed up he didn't no what state he was gov.of and trumps running mate pence is from indiana

Like · Reply · Message · July 29, 2016 at 9:13pm

████████████ Evidently *satire* press but I think they need new writers. I'll give it one "HA."

Like · Reply · Message · July 30, 2016 at 5:46am

William Goodspeed Thanks for the feedback. I'll put it in the writer's performance review (he's still in trouble for his holiday party antics). Thanks again.

Like · Reply · Message · July 30, 2016 at 10:49am

███████████ NO TAXES - NO VOTE FOR TRUMP

Like · Reply · Message · July 30, 2016 at 8:39am

█████████ Idiot!

Like · Reply · Message · July 30, 2016 at 6:56pm

████████████ Ok Trump miss spoke what about Kaines state is there higher taxes if so Trump was Right again

Like · Reply · Message · July 31, 2016 at 12:41pm

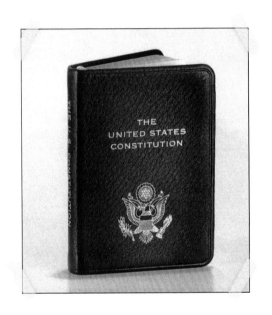

THIRTY-NINE

Trump Starts Apology Tour After Khan Controversy
August 2016

Satirical Press International (SPI), Columbus, Ohio —

Wolf Blitzer: Good afternoon, it's five o'clock on the East Coast, two o'clock Pacific. I'm reporting live from Columbus, Ohio, where it's also five o'clock, with Breaking News. We've just been told that in the wake of Donald Trump's criticism of Khizr and Ghazala Khan, Gold Star parents of fallen Captain Kahn, the Republican Presidential Nominee would embark on a tour of America to apologize for his statements. Who better to explain this than the candidate himself. Good afternoon, Mr. Trump.

Trump (*with signature scowl*): Afternoon, Wolf.

Blitzer: As you know, you have received considerable criticism about your comments related to the Kahn family, the parents of the fallen U.S. Muslim marine in Iraq.

Trump: They said some bad things about me at the Democratic convention, Wolf, very bad things. I don't know the Khans, never met them but still they stand on national TV, national TV, Wolf, and criticize me. If you hit me, Wolf, believe me, I'll hit back harder, trust me.

Blitzer: So is this the start of your apology tour?

Trump: I said that Captain Kahn was a hero — that's enough, though I prefer my heroes alive. His parents had no right to say all those things, no right.

Blitzer: What specifically did they say that bothered you? Was it that you never sacrificed anything? Was it about Muslin Americans? Or maybe the Constitution?

Trump: It's all false, Wolf, totally false. I've read the Constitution many times, many, many times, believe me. I probably know more about the Constitution than anyone in the world, trust me.

Blitzer: What's your favorite part?

Trump: There are so many — the Second Amendment is big, really big, very big — probably my favorite of the two amendments, but I'd have to say the most important part is about fighting the British and high taxes. We cannot tolerate foreigners taking jobs and our money, believe me, which is why we're going to build a wall and negotiate tough deals. If we have to throw Corona in Boston harbor, we'll do it, trust me.

Blitzer: You may be thinking of the Declaration of Independence.

Trump: I know what I'm saying, Wolf. I have a big brain, and by the way, the election is rigged. You watch. Everything is rigged, just like Debbie Wasserman Schultz and the DNC.

Blitzer: What do you say to Republican Speaker Paul Ryan, venerable Republican Senator and war hero John McCain and other prominent Republicans who say your criticism of the Khans was over-the-line?

Trump: Paul's a nice guy, but he's weak, so's McCain, which is why he got captured, by the way. I know a lot about this.

Blitzer: Many people say you are incapable of saying a kind word. What do you say to them?

Trump: That's an invention of the biased media, like you. I say kind words all the time.

Blitzer: Can you give an example?

Trump: I have a really high IQ.

Blitzer: How about an example about someone other than yourself?

Trump: Hmm, let me think — Vladimir Putin is a strong leader and shows what we need in the U.S.

Blitzer: We need Putin?

Trump: Strong leaders, not the weak like we've got now. President Obama is the worst U.S. President in history, believe me.

Blitzer: How about apologies? Do you ever apologize?

Trump: Of course.

Blitzer: Let's hear one.

Trump: I'm sorry Paul Ryan is such a loser. John McCain too. And Kelly Ayotte. I'm sorry she's not a strong person — America needs strong people, not weak ones. We need more Putins around here.

Blitzer: Thank you, Mr. Trump. Now we go back to the Situation Room with Pamela Brown, who will report on the Clinton campaign's surprise announcement that she no longer needs to campaign.

Facebook Comments to Article:

████████████ I don't trust this man with the lives of my children and grandchildren.
Like · Reply · Message · August 5, 2016 at 7:13pm

████████████ So you trust them with Hillary?
Like · Reply · Message · August 5, 2016 at 8:07pm

████████████ wake me when hillary goes an apology tour on her way to prison.
Like · Reply · Message · August 5, 2016 at 8:18pm

██████████ I trust Trump more than Hillary!!

Like · Reply · Message · August 5, 2016 at 9:08pm

██████████ Did u see the end where Blitzer had to go back for Hillary's surprise...she no longer needed to campaign? Now I wonder why?

Like · Reply · Message · August 5, 2016 at 10:13pm

██████████ At least one of them is starting to apologize!

Like · Reply · Message · August 5, 2016 at 10:30pm

██████████ Have enjoyed blocking the Trump trolls!!

Like · Reply · Message · August 5, 2016 at 11:02pm

██████████ BULLSHIT! HE DIDN'T APOLOGIZE. As for you jackass constitutional expert so am I. And you are an idiot. Obviously ignorant of the most sophisticated documents ever written. Obama taught Constitution law at Harvard and is is moron who can't spell his...*See More*

Like · Reply · Message · August 6, 2016 at 3:13am

██████████ Go Hillary go

Like · Reply · Message · August 6, 2016 at 6:07am

██████████ YOU TRUST A MAN WHO CAN'T TRUST HIMSELF!!!! HE HAS TO READ OFF A TELEPROMPTER OR A PIECE OF PAPER TO STAY WHAT SOMEONE ELSE TELLS HIM TO... AGAIN...WHAT SOMEONE ELSE TELLS HIM TO. LIKE A CHILD WHO IS TOLD TO SAY I'M SORRY TO A KID HE DOESN'T KNOW ON THE DAMN PLAYGROUND!!!! YOU KNOW DAMN WELL IF YOU DID IT... YOU DIDN'T MEAN IT!!! AND IF YOU WERE THE VICTIM... LATER ON... THE SAME BULLY... HE OR SHE DID IT AGAIN.

Like · Reply · Message · August 6, 2016 at 6:39am

██████████ HE IS EVERYTHING THAT MAKES AMERICA HATE.

Like · Reply · Message · August 6, 2016 at 6:40am

██████████████ He NEVER apologized and I doubt he ever will.

Like · Reply · Message · August 6, 2016 at 6:49am

██████████████ Apology tour ? My ass , I haven't heard him apologize to anyone. Last time I check they are called rallies..

Like · Reply · Message · August 6, 2016 at 7:35am

██████████████ To any moron voting for Clinton you need to read this! She is so corrupt and beyond fake! She takes fake to a new level! It is hilarious

Like · Reply · Message · August 6, 2016 at 9:09am

██████████████ Trump 2017 ♥

Like · Reply · Message · August 6, 2016 at 9:33am

██████████████ I think I should apologize for a small amount of things.. Other than that this is the Land of Free Speech...It is what is... He just says stuff that some won't but want to... It will be interesting month in Novemeber

Like · Reply · Message · August 6, 2016 at 10:38am

██████████████ Hillary Clinton has been unethical, and student of Communism since College days, tries to impress with out right lies, even when she knows there is news footage to prove she's lying!! Would trust den of Rattlesnakes more than world Champion liar!!

Like · Reply · Message · August 6, 2016 at 1:38pm

██████████████ Some people responding and haven't read the SATIRE

Like · Reply · Message · August 6, 2016 at 7:24pm

██████████████ ALERT TRUMP SUPPORTERS. IT WAS ANNOUNCED TODAY THAT HILLARY IS NOW ADVERTISING FOR PAID TROLLS. THIS IS WHAT IS HAPPENING HERE. THESE TROLLS WILL SAY ANYTHING FOR A BUCK.

Like · Reply · Message · August 6, 2016 at 9:33pm

████████ Don't see the constitution in your little hands!

Like · Reply · Message · August 7, 2016 at 2:59am

████████ Hes a nut case

Like · Reply · Message · August 6, 2016 at 11:13pm

████████ Anyone who thinks Hilary will begoodfor the future of our children is BLIND! And must be deaf also. !

Like · Reply · Message · August 7, 2016 at 7:16am

████████ Did anyone here notice this is satire....y'all too funny with bashing trump, you believe everything you read.....you my friends are part of the problem

Like · Reply · Message · August 7, 2016 at 1:45pm

████████ We don't have time for political correctness.

Like · Reply · Message · August 7, 2016 at 2:07pm

FORTY

Clinton Campaign Plans Layoffs, Vacations
August 2016

Satirical Press International — CNN's stunning anchor, Carol Costello, wearing her trademark glasses, opens her show from CNN's New York studios:

Costello: Newsroom starts now. Today, we will be covering the Breaking News that the Clinton Campaign is announcing hundreds of layoffs due to a steep drop-off in workload. We start with our own Jake Tapper, who is with Mrs. Clinton on Martha's Vineyard.

Tapper (*in an outdoor setting with a beach in the background across from Mrs. Clinton, who is hearing a hat, sunglasses and sipping an iced tea. She is intently reading something on her phone.*): Thanks, Carol. I'm here with Secretary Clinton on Martha's Vineyard. So, Madame Secretary, why with less than 90 days to go in the campaign, are you in Martha's Vineyard?

Clinton (*looks up from reading emails*): I'm just — you know — taking it easy, Jake. It's been a long haul, and I needed a vacation.

Tapper: But aren't you worried about taking time off in the middle of a pivotal campaign?

Clinton: Not at all. I planned on putting pedal to the metal the whole time, but Mr. Trump has dramatically reduced my need to campaign.

Tapper: How so?

Clinton: First came the fight with the Gold Star Khan family, followed by the Second Amendment implied call to arms to his supporters, then he called your network 'Crooked CNN' and today, he said Pennsylvania was rigged and people need to become electoral vigilantes.

Tapper: So, he's doing all the heavy lifting for you?

Clinton (*sipping her tea*): Exactamundo.

Tapper: Do you see any downside to this?

Clinton: Unfortunately, we have to lay off about half our staff — there's just no need for campaign help anymore. It's a shame, of course, but it's the only responsible thing to do.

Tapper: There you have it from Mrs. Clinton. Back to you in New York, Carol.

Costello: It sure looks nice there, Jake. Thanks for your report. For a reaction, we have our Political Correspondent, Dana Bash, with Donald Trump in Youngstown, Ohio.

Bash: Mr. Trump, you just heard Secretary Clinton's words, how do you respond?

Trump: She's a job killer. Our economy is stagnant, and she is destroying jobs. Half her campaign staff, folks. It won't happen under my watch, believe me, people will get new jobs, good jobs all over, trust me. In fact, my candidacy has already created thousands of good jobs, really good jobs across America.

Bash: Can you give an example?

Trump: Television comedy writing jobs and blogger positions are literally going through the roof.

Bash (*looking up*): Through the roof?

Trump: Literally.

Bash: Bloggers?

Trump: Yeah, it's incredible, all because of me. There's this blogger, William Goodspeed, who's hiring writers right and left. Most are happy for jobs because journalism is falling apart, folks, especially The New York Times, which is incredibly biased against my campaign, trust me. Probably the worst run paper in the world. Well, most of the hires are happy, except the interns.

Bash: Interns?

Trump: Yea, he has two unpaid interns from Northwestern University's journalism school — young ladies I think. They expected a fun summer of wining and dining and leisurely hours.

Bash: What happened?

Trump: I happened, that's what, and now they're working around the clock. They even called my campaign manager, pleading with him to make me stay on message.

Bash: Why?

Trump: Because every time I say something off the cuff — and I say great things off the cuff, by the way — they have to draft a new blog, which happens daily, trust me. I'll keep them so busy, they'll run back to Northwestern and transfer to nursing school, and not just because they're women, believe me. I love women, and women love me. All of them, especially my three wives. And Northwestern isn't as good a school as Wharton, where I went. If I were running that blog, I'd stock it with Ivy Leaguers, winners, trust me. Not losers like Goodspeed, who can't manage his way out of a bathroom, believe me.

Bash: Thank you for your insights, Mr. Trump. There you have it, Carol.

Costello (*looking perplexed and trying not to laugh*): Thanks, Dana. I just feel so bad for those interns.

Bash: Well, at least they have jobs, which is unusual for journalism students.

Facebook Comments to Article:

████████████ She announced at her rally yesterday that they were HIRING & told her people to apply for a job.
Like · Reply · Message · August 16, 2016 at 4:09am

████████████ That way she'll have more cash to hire actors to attend her rallies and register illigals and dead people to vote for her. lol
Like · Reply · Message · August 16, 2016 at 8:54am

████████████ She preparing for indictment...
http://www.worldnewspolitics.com/.../fbi-ignores-obama.../
Like · Reply · Message · August 16, 2016 at 12:50pm

████████████ She just said she wasn't taking anything for granted and she was fighting as hard as she ever did so whoever wrote this article is blowing smoke up people's rear ends
Like · Reply · Message · August 16, 2016 at 2:49pm

████████ Someone seriously needs to dress the woman. I love her, and am voting for her . But give Tim Gunn a call. She needs a style director.
Like · Reply · Message · August 16, 2016 at 3:06pm

████████ I'm afraid would be migraine instigator
Like · Reply · Message · August 16, 2016 at 6:02pm

████████████ Whenever Hillary announces a layoffs... I bet the people that are in line for the layoff are wondering if there going to end up Dead

Like · Reply · Message · August 16, 2016 at 9:41pm

████████████ People who thinks she is so need to open there eyes an start reading I like trump an not some body that is stuffing there pockets

Like · Reply · Message · August 16, 2016 at 9:46pm

████████████ Darrell, read what you wrote and ask yourself if it makes any sense

Like · Reply · Message · August 17, 2016 at 12:06am

████████████ That's her "witness protection apparel" for after the elections.....Trumps got this....

Like · Reply · Message · August 17, 2016 at 12:14am

████████ Trump is done, if she lays off people it's because she don't need them in the field. Usually they move their assets from strong states to weaker states but when a democrat is winning Arizona and Georgia where you going to send them?

Like · Reply · Message · August 17, 2016 at 12:31am

████████████ I believe this was meant as a joke

Like · Reply · Message · August 17, 2016 at 5:59am

████████████ Not real. It is a satire people.

Like · Reply · Message · August 17, 2016 at 5:57pm

████████████████ She needs a complete makeover and extreme surgery for that face. Lord please forgive.

Like · Reply · Message · August 17, 2016 at 9:13pm

FORTY-ONE

Biden-Clinton Tarmac Hug: Super Creepy
August 2016

Satirical Press International — It's 9 a.m. on the East Coast, and the CNN show, Newsday, opens with a new set. CNN's anchor, Carol Costello, wearing her trademark glasses, sits at a semi-circular table alongside a young, blonde woman.

Costello: Welcome to Newsday! We are proud to introduce Emma Jennings to our Newsday team. Emma is from Brentwood, California and is a recent graduate from UC Santa Barbara, where she majored in communications. This is part of a new effort by our show to bring views from important segments of our population, in this case millennials. Welcome, Emma.

Jennings: Thanks, Carol. I'm so excited to be here! You are, like, one of my idols, and I just love these cool studios.

Costello: I am honored, Emma. In our first story today, we'll explore what's been called The Hug, an awkward moment between Vice President Joe Biden and Secretary Hillary Clinton. On the tarmac at an airport in Pennsylvania, Biden met Clinton and gave her a seemingly endless hug.

Jennings: It was 16 seconds, Carol!

Costello: As a young female millennial, what do you think about The Hug?

Jennings: It was super creepy. I was, like, freaking out when I saw it.

Costello: So you wouldn't welcome such a hug from the Vice President?

Jennings: OMG, no! I'm afraid he'd, like, stalk me on Facebook.

Costello: Well, Emma, let's see how the Right and the Left reacted to The Hug. We're now talking live with former Pennsylvania Senator and Republican presidential candidate Rick Santorum. What did you think of The Hug, Senator?

Santorum: That kind of thing shouldn't be on television, Carol. Unless such a hug is part of the miracle of human reproduction, it shouldn't happen.

Costello: Emma?

Jennings (*with a look of horror on her face*): I've got a picture in my head, and it's, like, super gross.

Costello (*laughing*): Thanks, Senator. For another view, we have none other than Secretary Clinton herself, along with a campaign aide. So, Mrs. Clinton, the Internet is abuzz about The Hug. Did you enjoy it?

Clinton: Vice President Biden has been one of the best Vice Presidents we've ever had. He's a man of the people with an inspiring story. And great teeth.

Costello: But how did you enjoy The Hug?

Clinton: It lasted a little too long for being on camera, but it was kind of nice. I haven't had a nice loving hug from a man since. . . . (*turning to her aide*). How old is Chelsea?

Costello (*in tears laughing*): Thank you, Madame Secretary. Well, Emma, what do you think?

Jennings: I'm super grossed out. I just need to sit in my cubicle and chill.

Facebook Comments to Article:

████████████ CREEPY CREEPY
Like · Reply · Message · August 20, 2016 at 12:57pm

████████████ TWO PIGS KISSING.
Like · Reply · Message · August 20, 2016 at 3:10pm

████████████ Ewwwwww
Like · Reply · Message · August 20, 2016 at 4:45pm

████████ Creepy
Like · Reply · Message · August 20, 2016 at 5:35pm

████████████ mind your own busines ! wait til you are being caught in an akward moment
Like · Reply · Message · August 20, 2016 at 7:04pm

████████████ Cosey
Like · Reply · Message · August 20, 2016 at 7:09pm

████████████ Hugging Biden and kissing Obama!!! My goodness who is next?
Like · Reply · Message · August 20, 2016 at 8:14pm

████████ Uncle Joe is pulling Her up on the Blue V#%n Throbber ....
Like · Reply · Message · August 20, 2016 at 11:53pm

████████████ Y do people think because they hugged there something wrong with it n u make it dirty Shane on u if it was any one else hugging you would not think any thing is wrong with it because its Hillary Clinton so quick to judge
Like · Reply · Message · August 21, 2016 at 8:38am

████████████ Because if that had been President Trump doing the hugging on ANYONE like that the Communist News Network would run a two week long attack piece accusing Trump of being a perv. The libtard double standard is truly a sad thing...
Like · Reply · Message · August 21, 2016 at 10:54am

█████ Who gives a f--k!
Like · Reply · Message · August 21, 2016 at 11:15am

███████ If you find a problem in a hug from a good man, it's all on you.
Like · Reply · Message · August 21, 2016 at 11:44am

█████████ Just plain "in a daze" WEIRD !
Like · Reply · Message · August 21, 2016 at 12:31pm

████████ Hugging a friend is not news worthy
Like · Reply · Message · August 21, 2016 at 1:58pm

██████ Oh geezzzz, really? Boy can people make something out of nothing! Get a grip!
Like · Reply · Message · August 21, 2016 at 3:59pm

████████ Now that is one sexy couple!!
Like · Reply · Message · August 21, 2016 at 6:02pm

███████ Hillary Clinton suffered a brain injury in 2012 when she passed out and fell down and hit her head. She is suffering from a blood clot between her brain and her skull. She will have to take blood thinners for the rest of her life. The black man standin...*See More*
Like · Reply · Message · August 22, 2016 at 12:40am

William Goodspeed Thank you all for reading my blog and making comments. I always appreciate it. So you know, I try to satirize current events, primarily for entertainment and a few laughs. This blog is not meant to criticize Joe Biden, whom I like, or hugs (I like them too), but makes light of the way young people talk, how the far right reacts to things and the Clinton marriage.
Like · Reply · Message · August 22, 2016 at 8:17am

FORTY-TWO

Clinton Foundation Closeout Sale
August 2016

Donald J. Trump ✔
@realDonaldTrump

"Clinton Foundation's Fundraisers Pressed Donors to Steer Business to Former President"

7:12 AM - 27 Oct 2016

9,236 retweets 15,408 likes

Donald J. Trump ✔
@realDonaldTrump

'Hillary's Two Official Favors To Morocco Resulted In $28 Million For Clinton Foundation' #DrainTheSwamp

9:00 AM - 31 Oct 2016 from Chicago, IL

1,857 replies 14,566 retweets 23,198 likes

Donald J. Trump ✔
@realDonaldTrump

Saudi Arabia and many of the countries that gave vast amounts of money to the Clinton Foundation- cont'd:

2:32 PM - 13 Jun 2016

1,360 replies 6,881 retweets 14,610 likes

Satirical Press International —

Wolf Blitzer: It's 5 p.m. on the East Coast. I'm Wolf Blitzer in CNN's Situation Room in Washington D.C. We're covering Breaking News, possibly big enough to turn media attention away from Donald Trump. According to reports from the Associated Press, The Clinton Foundation has decided to quit accepting money from foreign donors, even from democratic countries. Tonight, we're going up close and personal with former President Bill Clinton, who is the founder of the Clinton Foundation. Good afternoon, Mr. President.

Clinton: Hey, Wolf, it's good to be on the show.

Blitzer: Can you explain the decision to quit accepting foreign donations? Is it because it makes both Democrats and Republicans very uneasy? Or do you think this addresses concerns about your wife's ethics?

Clinton: Wolf, just to be clear, we are still accepting foreign donations.

Blitzer: Really?

Clinton: Right up until the minute Hillary gets elected.

Blitzer: What message do you hope to send with this announcement?

Clinton (*looking seriously into the camera*): For our foreign donors, you only have a limited time to give. This offer closes in November — we won't even have our annual Black Friday sale — so buy now.

Blitzer: So up until the election, the Foundation can accept tens of millions, even hundreds of millions, from all kinds of foreign donors?

Clinton: With the clock ticking, we're hoping for a surge in giving, Wolf. The likely prospect of Hillary becoming the most powerful person in the world also makes this a compelling offer.

Blitzer: So if, say, a Russian billionaire kleptocrat gave the Foundation $200 million, Secretary Clinton would forget about it if she was elected?

Clinton: Once Hillary takes office, she will delete everything. She knows how to do it.

Blitzer: How about you, Mr. President? Assuming you are not in the cabinet, would you continue to solicit donations?

Clinton: Absolutely not — I would focus on speaking fees.

Blitzer: Like the $17 million you received from Laureate University?

Clinton: You can't blame me, Wolf, it's the market price, and besides, I have a family to feed.

Blitzer: Does this hurt the Clinton credibility about fixing the economy and helping the middle class?

Clinton: Quite the opposite, Wolf.

Blitzer: How so?

Clinton: Cinderella story — if we can make hundreds of millions without producing anything, so can anybody. It's the American dream.

Facebook Comments to Article:

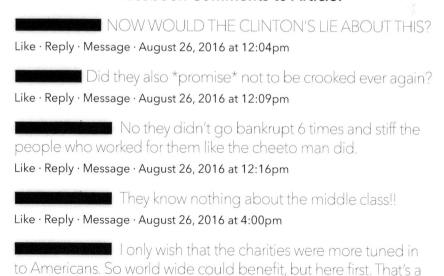

████████████ NOW WOULD THE CLINTON'S LIE ABOUT THIS?
Like · Reply · Message · August 26, 2016 at 12:04pm

████████ Did they also *promise* not to be crooked ever again?
Like · Reply · Message · August 26, 2016 at 12:09pm

████████ No they didn't go bankrupt 6 times and stiff the people who worked for them like the cheeto man did.
Like · Reply · Message · August 26, 2016 at 12:16pm

████████████ They know nothing about the middle class!!
Like · Reply · Message · August 26, 2016 at 4:00pm

████████████ I only wish that the charities were more tuned in to Americans. So world wide could benefit, but here first. That's a conflict in my mind. Nice sentiment but out of focus.

Like · Reply · Message · August 26, 2016 at 4:40pm

████████████ Sounds good. The most important thing for helping prevent slavery overseas is security. That's what foreign donars are buying. Anyone can hire doctors and nurses and teachers and build clinics and schools. But without security it is a waste of time...*See More*

Like · Reply · Message · August 26, 2016 at 4:53pm

████████████ Throw then in jail

Like · Reply · Message · August 26, 2016 at 4:00pm

████████████ They're liars and thieves. 😡 😡 😡

Like · Reply · Message · August 27, 2016 at 3:50am

████████████ You cant believe one word any of the CLINTONS say...They live off off lies ,deceit,and thievery.

Like · Reply · Message · August 27, 2016 at 12:52pm

██████████████ What Clinton credibility???

Like · Reply · Message · August 27, 2016 at 5:09pm

████████████ Nauseating !!

Like · Reply · Message · August 27, 2016 at 5:54pm

████████████ people are,so blinded the good they have done far outweighs the bad , these people have Been dogged an crucified by Republicans for years an the worst part they have committed far worse schemes an lies,an being crooked than the Clintons have ever done

Like · Reply · Message · August 27, 2016 at 8:52pm

████████████ Put this one in the pile of missing emails.

Like · Reply · Message · August 27, 2016 at 11:23pm

FORTY-THREE

Trump Wannabe: Maine Governor Paul LePage
August 2016

Satirical Press International — CNN's charming anchor, Carol Costello, opens her show, Newsroom, at 9 a.m.:

Costello: This time of year, Maine is known as Vacationland, home to the Bush family, lobster rolls and beautiful coastline. Vacationland's late summer bliss was shattered this week by a volatile argument over racism. For a full report, we go to idyllic Bar Harbor with our political correspondent, Pamela Brown. Good morning, Pamela.

Brown: Good morning, Carol, from beautiful Bar Harbor, full of tourists and cruise ships. I'm here with Jacques Sangfroid, the spokesman for Maine Governor, Paul LePage. Good day to you, sir.

Sangfroid: Good morning, Pamela. Welcome to Vacationland.

Brown: Thank you. Well, it's been quite a week for your boss, Governor LePage. A few days ago, he left a voicemail for a state legislator. Let me read part of it for you:

"I want to talk to you. I want you to prove that I'm a racist. I've spent my life helping black people and you little son-of-a-bitch, socialist cocksucker. You...I need you to, just friggin. I want you to record this and make it

public because I am after you. Thank you."

What's your reaction to this?

Sangfroid: It was nice of him to end by saying 'thank you.'

Brown: What about the expletives and other parts of the message?

Sangfroid: Well, Pamela, any statement can be made to sound bad if you take it out of context.

Brown: What context is that?

Sangfroid: Governor LePage had been called a racist, the worst word ever.

Brown: Apparently, the Governor found some other bad words. How do you respond to charges that the Governor is racist?

Sangfroid: The Governor refuses to be politically correct—he's like Donald Trump without the hair.

Brown: That's fair to say. Let me read another quote for you that some have described as racist. In it, he is describing heroin traffickers that he says are 90% black or Hispanic:

"They come up here, they sell their heroin, then they go back home. Incidentally, half the time they impregnate a young white girl before they leave."

Sangfroid: He's a very strong person and stands up for what's right.

Brown: Is that why he said he wished it was the year 1825 so he could challenge the legislator to a pistol duel?

Sangfroid: He was just making a statement. In the Governor's mind, it's not 1825. He knows it's 1950, um, I mean 2016.

Facebook Comments to Article:

███████████ He is crazy !
Like · Reply · Message · August 31, 2016 at 11:37am

███████████ Yes, if I had to guess, I would say he's a little upset !!!!
Like · Reply · Message · August 31, 2016 at 5:34pm

███████████ No problem, just a rise in temperature. Lol
Like · Reply · Message · August 31, 2016 at 6:43pm

███████████ Idiot!!!!,
Like · Reply · Message · August 31, 2016 at 8:32pm

███████████ ANOTHER IDIOT.
Like · Reply · Message · September 1, 2016 at 10:53am

███████████ IDIOT!!
Like · Reply · Message · September 1, 2016 at 7:59pm

███████████ He was Trump before Trump was Trump!
Like · Reply · Message · September 1, 2016 at 8:29pm

███████████ Take a little part of a story and share to get the reaction you want.
Like · Reply · Message · September 2, 2016 at 4:29am

███████████ He will only retire if Trump can find him a position..........
Like · Reply · Message · September 2, 2016 at 7:11am

███████████ Oh dear god
Like · Reply · Message · September 2, 2016 at 7:57am

FORTY-FOUR

Mexico to Build Wall
September 2016

Satirical Press International — In the wake of Republican Presidential Candidate Donald Trump's brief visit to Mexico, the country's young president, Enrique Peña Nieto, holds a press conference for American journalists in Mexico City. Standing behind a podium surrounded by Mexican flags, President Peña Nieto addresses a group of journalists:

Peña Nieto: "Good afternoon, amigos and amigas, and Bienvenidos a Mexico. We enjoy having our cousins from the North. Let's take the first question. Mr. Blitzer from CNN, I'll start with you because I watch The Situation Room on CNN International."

Wolf Blitzer: "Thank you, Mr. President. Can you comment on your meeting yesterday with Donald Trump? Did you discuss the proposed wall between our countries? Will Mexico pay for the wall?"

Peña Nieto: "Which question would you like me to answer?"

Blitzer: "How did it go with Mr. Trump?"

Peña Nieto: "Overall, I must say it was cordial, but we had disagreements on some major issues."

George Stephanopoulos (ABC): "Did you disagree about who would pay for the wall?"

Peña Nieto: "No, we did not even agree on who would build the wall."

George Stephanopoulos (ABC): "Is Mexico offended by Mr. Trump's idea to build a wall?"

Peña Nieto: "Not at all, *señor*. In fact, after careful thought, Mexico has decided that we want to build a wall on the U.S. border."

Bill O'Reilly (Fox): "Mexico wants to build a wall? Is that to save face and not have to succumb to American pressure from Mr. Trump?"

Peña Nieto: "No, *Señor* O'Reilly. We watch CNN everyday — no offense — and worry much about the American election."

O'Reilly: "Are you worried Hillary Clinton will win?"

Peña Nieto: "To be truthful, we worry if anyone wins. It's like choosing between death by poison and getting shot."

Lester Holt (NBC): "Which is worse?"

Peña Nieto: "Both are bad, *Señor Holt*. We expect millions of refugees after the election. Millions."

Holt: "What kind of refugees?"

Peña Nieto: "If Trump wins, we will have millions of liberals coming to Mexico making us feel guilty about gluten in our *tortillas*. That would be intolerable! Though we welcome immigrants, we worry about losing our culture. But if Clinton wins, we have another big problem — how would we handle all the diehard Trump supporters? We don't even have a single NASCAR track."

Holt: "Are there other reasons why Mexico wants to build a wall?"

Peña Nieto: "*Si, Señor Holt*. If the U.S. builds a wall, we think it will not be tasteful. We prefer a nice adobe style structure, something to be proud about, maybe a nice fresco mural."

O'Reilly: "What about the cost? Mr. Trump estimates the wall could cost $20 billion."

Peña Nieto: "You're forgetting we have millions of inexpensive construction workers. Our costs will be far less, which is another reason we don't want America to build it."

Holt: "Aren't you afraid Americans will just buy ladders and climb over the wall?"

Peña Nieto (*looking worriedly at his aides*): "Um, we hadn't thought of that. Let me get back to you on that one."

Stephanopoulos: "Did you have any other impressions of Donald Trump?"

Peña Nieto: "*Si,* he has very small hands. I've had *quesadillas* a lot bigger.

Facebook Comments to Article:

████████████ THAT IS BETTER YET JUST SO IT IS A SECURE WALL AND WE WILL PUT OUR MAN POWER ON THIS SIDE ! MAKE SURE IT IS NOT ABLE TO HAVE TUNNELS ETC WELL MEXICO GO AHEAD PAY FOR THE WALL AS LONG AS IT MEATS TRUMPS SPECKS FOR THIS COUNTRY !

Like · Reply · Message · September 7, 2016 at 1:48pm

████████████ Mr.Trump said they were. 😄 Hahahahaha hahahaha!

Like · Reply · Message · September 7, 2016 at 4:28pm

████████████ Thats another way to get them to pay for it

Like · Reply · Message · September 7, 2016 at 7:37pm

████████████ They must be worried all the ones who say they will leave USA when Trump wins.Read the article,ghe comments of his last statements are entertaining lol

Like · Reply · Message · September 7, 2016 at 9:15pm

████████████ Amusing....

Like · Reply · Message · September 7, 2016 at 10:48pm

████████████ A Big No on that one.

Like · Reply · Message · September 8, 2016 at 2:44am

████████████ No Mexico will not pay for a wall..they can't even pay to clean up their own government n police...horrid country especially if you're a woman

Like · Reply · Message · September 8, 2016 at 3:17am

████████████ Look up definition of satire,political satire. Ha ha.

Like · Reply · Message · September 8, 2016 at 3:26am

████████████ Will we also get our factories back that left us high and dry just so they could have cheaper labor and we would get cheaper quality back in return?

Like · Reply · Message · September 8, 2016 at 8:26am

████████████ Because of Trump's visit an assistant to the Mexican President was asked to resign because he had set up the visit. The people of Mexico hate Trump and the president has been under constant attack and fired.

Like · Reply · Message · September 8, 2016 at 8:51am

████████████ If I was Mexico I want a wall, a really big one. With even the slightest possibility of someone like Trump in charge of anything, I'd want to be as far away as possible too. And they can't move the whole country. As of right now I'm still proud to be an American. Trump could ruin everything.

Like · Reply · Message · September 8, 2016 at 1:01pm

████████████ Do you people really believe this garbage.

Like · Reply · Message · September 8, 2016 at 4:13pm

Source: Twitter@PutinRF__Eng March 1, 2017

FORTY-FIVE

Vladimir Putin: New American Idol
September 2016

 Donald J. Trump ✓
@realDonaldTrump

Great move on delay (by V. Putin) - I always knew he was very smart!

11:41 AM - 30 Dec 2016

35,172 replies   34,404 retweets   97,625 likes

Satirical Press International — "Good morning, this is Matt Lauer of The Today Show, live from Studio 3B in New York. Today, we're going deep into the heartland to learn about American attitudes toward Russian President Vladimir Putin, which has become a hot topic since Donald Trump and Mike Pence have expressed admiration for his leadership. For this, we go to Grand Rapids, Michigan, where Savannah Guthrie is with South Grand Rapids High School's Class of 1976 at their 40th reunion."

The tall and lean Savannah Guthrie stands before a group of five women wearing nametags in front of South Grand Rapids High School. A large group is standing behind them holding several signs and shaking pompoms.

Guthrie: Good morning, Matt! I'm with an excited group of South

Grand Rapids alumni today here in Michigan. How are you ladies?

First woman (*Sally*): Just fantastic, Savannah. Go Homesteaders!!!!

Guthrie: Homesteaders?

Sally: You betcha! That's our mascot. We're the South GR Homesteaders, and we're not just settlers! (huge cheers from the crowd with Homesteader signs waving)

Guthrie: I understand it's your 40th reunion, and you're playing your big rival tonight, the East Grand Rapids Pioneers.

Crowd: BEAT THE PIONEERS, BEAT THEM SENSELESS!

Guthrie: It's great to hear that kind of spirit here in America. On another topic, what do you ladies think of Vladimir Putin?

Second woman (*Jane*): He's a very strong man and leader.

Guthrie: So you approve of him?

Jane: Don't tell my husband, but when I see pictures of President Putin riding a horse shirtless, it takes me places I've never been before.

Guthrie (*to the group*): Do you all agree?

Group: Woo hoo, we do! Go Homesteaders, Beat the Pioneers!!!!!

Guthrie: Do you know that Putin has become a billionaire and he's an alleged kleptomaniac?

Jane: We don't discriminate against people suffering from kleptomaniacism; it's un-American.

Guthrie: I see. What else do you all like about President Putin?

Third woman (*Julie*): He plays a tough sport like hockey. Can I say hi to my husband, Dirk, in Kalamazoo? He loves The Today Show.

Guthrie: Go right ahead.

Julie: Hi Honey! I'll try to get Savannah's autograph. She's really tall!

Guthrie: So you like that he plays hockey?

Julie: It's a man's sport. You'll never find President Putin playing golf in Martha's Vineyard, like our so-called president.

Guthrie: You're right about that. Does it bother any of you that President Putin has been accused of jailing or killing journalists who criticize him?

Julie: Heck no! He stands up to the liberal media, like a real man. Um, no offense, Savannah.

Guthrie: None taken; I get it all the time. There you have it from South Grand Rapids, Matt.

Crowd: GO HOMESTEADERS!!!!!

Matt: Thanks, Savannah. After this short break, we have a special segment on how Hollywood celebrities deal with wrinkles.

 Hillary Clinton ✓
@HillaryClinton

We don't know why Trump and Putin praise each other so much and share many foreign policies. We'll let you guess.

5:50 AM - 5 Aug 2016

2,031 replies 7,966 retweets 12,637 likes

 Hillary Clinton ✓
@HillaryClinton

At last night's forum, Trump disrespected our generals, our country, and women in the military—but he praised Putin.

11:07 AM - 8 Sep 2016

1,527 replies 6,370 retweets 10,524 likes

Donald J. Trump ✓
@realDonaldTrump

Vladimir Putin said today about Hillary and Dems: "In my opinion, it is humiliating. One must be able to lose with dignity." So true!

4:13 PM - 23 Dec 2016

34,814 replies   31,736 retweets   112,919 likes

Facebook Comments to Article:

████████████ I love Vlad and he is a better leader than Oslimey

Like · Reply · Message · September 14, 2016 at 6:10pm

████████████ What an odd thing to say.

Like · Reply · Message · September 14, 2016 at 6:51pm

████████████ Are you people crazy, this man would love to see America destroyed

Like · Reply · Message · September 14, 2016 at 9:09pm

████████████ He's creepy...... Yuk!

Like · Reply · Message · September 14, 2016 at 10:08pm

████████████ He is 10X the man.

Like · Reply · Message · June 28, 2016 at 7:58am

Source: Twitter@KimJongUnique

FORTY-SIX

Kim Jong Un Has Putin Envy
September 2016

Satirical Press International — CNN's morning anchor, Carol Costello, opens her show, Newsday, with a stunning announcement:

Costello: "Good morning and thank you for joining us this morning. In Breaking News today, we have just learned that North Korea detonated a nuclear bomb overnight. Coincidentally, our new millennial correspondent, Emma Jennings, is in Pyongyang this week to interview North Korean President Kim Jong Un, which was recorded a few hours ago. Emma, good evening to you! How are things in North Korea?"

Jennings: "Carol, this place is, like, oh my God! My Instagram account has been blocked, and I'm like freaking out. And I'm dying for my daily soy latte ice coffee at Starbucks. There are like no Starbucks here."

Costello: "We'll have a Starbucks binge when you get back, Emma, but we sent you there as a young single American woman to get to know President Kim Jong Un, who has been touted as the world's most eligible bachelor dictator. What have you learned?"

Jennings: "I'm down with that, Carol. We had a great chat this morning, by the way."

Costello: "Let's play the interview now."

Jennings (*seated across from Kim Jong Un and his interpreter*): "President Kim, thank you for giving me the honor of being the first American journalist to interview you."

Kim (*via interpreter*): "It's my pleasures, Miss Jenning."

Jennings: "According to rumor, you are upset that American presidential candidate Donald Trump keeps praising Vladimir Putin of Russia but never mentions you. Some say you have 'Putin Envy'. Is this true?"

Kim (*through interpreter*): "I am some very strong leader — they call me The Supreme Leader — but Mr. Trumps does not offer me respects."

Jennings: "What do you plan to do about it?"

Kim (*through interpreter*): "For starters, I exploded some nuclear weapon last night. Big bang, earthquakes, the whole — how you say — nachos!"

Jennings: "You mean *enchilada*?"

Kim (*through interpreter*): "Yes, sorry, we have no Taco Bells in North Korea."

Jennings: "Or Starbucks, President Kim, to be totally, like, honest. Let's help the world get to know the real Supreme Leader. When you're not plotting the death of millions from nuclear destruction, what do you enjoy doing?"

Kim: "I like to have my generals executed. Just last months, I had one generals killed for falling asleeps in my meetings."

Jennings: "It sounds like a Starbucks in Pyongyang would be really handy, at least for the generals. What about your social life? Do you have a girlfriend? Women around the world want to know."

Kim: "I have met some nice girl on Matches.com."

Jennings: "As a famous dictator, you certainly could date celebrities. Do you have any in mind?"

Kim: "To be some honest, I would very much like to marry Kim Kardashians. She is very beautiful."

Jennings: "Do you know that if she married you, her name would be Kim Kim?"

Kim (*laughing*): "I would name some new bomb after her — the Kim Kim Bomb."

Jennings: "That would be, like, super romantic. No one has, like, ever done that for me."

Kim: "You live in wrong countries, Ms. Jenning."

Jennings: "But I gotta, like, have my daily Starbucks."

Kim: "We can make Starbuck here by tomorrow." (*Kim issues command to general on the side*)

Jennings: "You probably say that to, like, all the girls."

Kim: "Just remember: Vladimir Putin can't have a Kim Kim."

Jennings: "No, I guess he couldn't."

Kim: "I am some very strong leader, and we do not let some Mexican in here. Please tell your Mr. Trumps."

Jennings: "I will."

Kim: "From now ons, if he mention me instead of Putin, I will send him some hat that say 'Make North Korea Greats Again.'"

Jennings: "That's, like, a super sweet offer. Thanks for your time, President Kim."

Kim: "My pleasant. Please let me know if there is anythings I can do for you."

Jennings (*pulling out a selfie stick*): "Do you mind doing a selfie with me?"

Kim: "Does Dennis Rodman have many piercing?"

Jennings (*takes selfie and starts uploading*) "That's, like, sooo funny. Hey, are you on Facebook?"

FORTY-SEVEN

Tweeting at 3 a.m.
October 2016

 Alicia Machado ✓
@machadooficial

Ex-Miss Universe: Trump Called Me 'Miss Piggy' -- The Cut @ NYMag

4:37 PM - 19 May 2016

3 retweets 14 likes

 Hillary Clinton ✓
@HillaryClinton

Donald Trump called her "Miss Piggy" and "Miss Housekeeping." Her name is Alicia Machado. #DebateNight

8:33 PM - 26 Sep 2016

3,026 replies 64,169 retweets 86,386 likes

 Hillary Clinton ✓
@HillaryClinton

The tools Donald Trump brings to the table—bragging, mocking, composing nasty tweets—won't do the trick.

12:22 PM - 2 Jun 2016

838 replies 1,929 retweets 4,481 likes

Satirical Press International — CNN's Anderson Cooper opens his show, Anderson Cooper 360°, with big news:

Cooper: Good evening. I'm Anderson Cooper, and this is Anderson Cooper 360°.

Cooper: Just days after the contentious presidential debate, Republican candidate Donald Trump has lashed out against Hillary Clinton in a series of late night Tweets. Tonight, we have an exclusive interview with the candidate. Good evening, Mr. Trump.

Trump (*scowling at the camera*): Good evening, Cooper.

Cooper: First, how did you feel after the first debate?

Trump: It was a great performance, totally great, believe me. Hillary Clinton showed she's not just Crooked Hillary — she's boring, trust me. Very boring. If not for my sniffles, I would have fallen asleep from boredom. All the talk about policies — yawn. Reminded me of some professors at Wharton, where I went, which is Ivy League, by the way, a great school, trust me.

Cooper: About the sniffles, what was going on?

Trump: I had a bad microphone — Lester Holt and the debate organizers, who are Democrats, set me up, trust me. It's part of the liberal media bias.

Cooper: Lester Holt is a registered Republican.

Trump: Just because someone registers as a Republican, doesn't mean they're a Republican. He's a Democrat, through and through.

Cooper: Because he's an African-American?

Trump: And he's in the liberal media. I can add 2 plus 2, believe me. I have a very large brain, very large.

Cooper: Back to the sniffles. How do feel?

Trump: Never better, Anderson, trust me. There's never been a healthier candidate for president. You don't see me with pneumonia and almost fainting, you'll never see it. Never. Ask my doctor, he knows. I'm a model of health, believe me. Robust health. Secretary Clinton can't walk 15 feet to her car, can't even make it. It's a total disaster.

Cooper: Are you having trouble sleeping these days?

Trump: Not at all, believe me. I've got great stamina and don't need much sleep, not much at all. In fact, I sleep less than anyone who's ever run for office, trust me. That's why I'll always be ready to take the call for America and respond with a Tweet.

Cooper: Recently, you Tweeted at 3 a.m. about Miss Universe 1996, Alicia Machado, saying she had weight issues.

Trump: Big ones, really big ones, trust me. She won the title and immediately strapped on the feed bag. It was a disaster, total disaster, believe me.

Cooper: I just saw a picture of her on Twitter — she's stunning.

Trump: She was Miss Piggy, trust me.

Cooper: But according to your doctor, you weigh 240 pounds. Isn't it hypocritical for you to criticize a woman's weight?

Trump: I'm a guy, okay? Machado is a girl who was elected Miss Universe, not some slob like Rosie O'Donnell, who everyone in America hates, everyone, trust me. Women should be thin. All my wives have been fit, very fit.

Cooper: What were you doing awake at 3 a.m.?

Trump: I drink warm milk, okay? It calms me down, not that I need calming down — I have the best temperament for president in our history. No one has had such a winning temperament, believe me. No one. Those who say otherwise are losers, total losers! When I become president, they'll experience my temperament first hand.

Cooper: You obviously hadn't had your warm milk before Tweeting. On another topic, Mrs. Clinton accused you of stiffing middle class workers who labored for your companies in Atlantic City —

Trump: They did bad work, very bad work. They were a disaster.

Cooper: Specifically, Mrs. Clinton and others have mentioned the middle class man who built the separators in the bathroom stalls — that he didn't get paid for the job he did.

Trump: He got paid what it was worth, which was zilch. His work was very poor, very low quality.

Cooper: You personally inspected his bathroom work?

Trump: I spend a lot of time in the bathrooms, Cooper, a lot of time. Didn't you watch the debate?

Cooper: Of course, but what does that have to do with the bathroom?

Trump: I drink a lot of water, okay?

**Donald Trump
has paid $0
in taxes before.
He might be still.***

*We don't know for sure,
 because he won't release
 his tax returns.

Source: @Hillary Clinton, August 12, 2016

FORTY-EIGHT

Taxes and Financial Genius
October 2016

Donald J. Trump ✓
@realDonaldTrump

In interview I told @AP that my taxes are under routine audit and I would release my tax returns when audit is complete, not after election!

1:51 PM - 11 May 2016

3,433 replies   4,881 retweets   15,332 likes

Hillary Clinton ✓
@HillaryClinton

After his lawyers advised against it, Trump used a "legally dubious" strategy to avoid paying taxes for years.

8:06 AM - 1 Nov 2016

2,028 replies   3,462 retweets   5,441 likes

Satirical Press International — CNN's bespectacled morning anchor, Carol Costello, moves to the first segment of her morning show, Newsroom:

Costello: As has been reported by the New York Times, Donald Trump's

1995 personal tax return shows a deduction for a loss of over 915 million dollars. According to tax experts, this loss could have allowed Mr. Trump to legally avoid paying taxes for 18 years. So what do you think of this? Let's talk. Today, we have Trump surrogate and former New York Mayor, Rudy Giuliani, tax expert Robert Clawson, and civil rights advocate from Louisiana, Mae Du Bois. (*the camera shows all three at a semi-circular table facing Ms. Costello*) Let's start with Mayor Giuliani. What do you make of the Trump tax return?

Giuliani: It shows the brilliance of Donald Trump, plain and simple.

Costello: Brilliance?

Giuliani: Of course, who else could think of ways to go two decades without paying federal income tax? The man is a financial genius, just what our country needs, not some woman.........um, person who has only created jobs in the FBI for agents investigating her.

Costello: Woman, huh? Isn't this just another loophole that Mr. Trump is using to take advantage of America?

Giuliani: Absolutely not. It's every American's patriotic duty to pay as little tax as possible. That's what makes America great.

Costello: Like in Italy, where income tax laws are considered a recommendation?

Giuliani: My ethnicity should not be an issue in this discussion, Carol.

Costello: Okay, Mr. Clawson, you are a tax partner with a major accounting firm and have worked in the field for 30 years. Can you answer the question — is Mr. Trump acting legally?

Clawson: I don't have all the returns, but from the looks of it, Mr. Trump is using what's called a 'net operating loss carry forward' to shield his taxes after 1995.

Costello: Sounds a bit dodgy to me, can you explain?

Clawson: Yes, if a taxpayer loses money in a given year, he or she can spread the unused loss over future years as a deduction from income taxes. It's perfectly legal.

Costello: Hmm. What do you think of this argument, Ms. Du Bois?

Du Bois: It's ridiculous, just another way the rich soak the poor in this country.

Costello: Can you explain?

Du Bois: If I was a working class woman of color, do you think I could get away with a $915 million deduction? No way.

(*Giuliani and Clawson look at Du Bois with dismay*)

Costello: I suppose it would be difficult.

Du Bois: Damn straight it would be.

Costello: Mr. Clawson, do you agree?

Clawson: Yes, anyone with middle class income who claims $915 million in business losses would probably receive extra IRS scrutiny.

Du Bois: See? Even the pros agree with me. Thanks, Bob.

Clawson: Don't mention it, Mae.

Costello: Well, apart from the tax aspects of this, does Mr. Trump's return reveal anything relevant to his candidacy?

Giuliani: Sheer genius and financial sophistication, like I said.

Costello: Can you explain how such a huge loss is evidence of financial genius?

Giuliani: You can't lose a billion dollars unless you have a billion dollars. Who better to watch over our $17 trillion economy?

Facebook Comments to Article:

▮▮▮▮▮▮▮▮▮▮ A non issue period...no one has shown it to be illegal... Some of these people would tell their tax accountant not to take the deductions they are allowed and pay the full tax...right? What a joke!

Like · Reply · Message · October 6, 2016 at 11:52am

▮▮▮▮▮▮▮▮▮▮ Show all the returns ,a majority of 916 million he lost was investors money not his own but claimed it as a personal loss.

Like · Reply · Message · October 6, 2016 at 12:05pm

▮▮▮▮▮▮▮▮▮ Oh baloney I has to do the same exact thing years ago just to survive and take care of my family. It WASN'T directly Trump's fault and he rebuilt and hired thousands of people...wake up !!

Like · Reply · Message · October 6, 2016 at 1:00pm

▮▮▮▮▮▮▮▮▮ Well done Speed and you have inspired some insightful feedback. 😊

Like · Reply · Message · October 6, 2016 at 3:36pm

▮▮▮▮▮▮▮▮▮▮ Absolutely, if you are business owner, you go through lean times, especially start-up. Losses carried forward allows you to repair the damage with future income. Big businesses do it all the time as well, why do you think sometimes even GE pays an effe...*See More*

Like · Reply · Message · October 6, 2016 at 3:49pm

▮▮▮▮▮▮▮▮ Small businesses have gone out of business. BUT HIS KLANCY DADDY BAILED HIM OUT OVER AND OVER!!! Said it on TV. Everytime he lost money he called his daddy for a loan. Every time.

Like · Reply · Message · October 6, 2016 at 8:53pm

▮▮▮▮▮▮▮▮▮ William Goodspeed , Clinton purposefully brought it up because small minds don't understand it and think that there

is something wrong with it!!...Got it?...... I didn't think so.......
HA HA HA......
Like · Reply · Message · October 6, 2016 at 11:33pm

▓▓▓▓▓▓▓ Blame Congress for making laws that make all
this legal.
Like · Reply · Message · October 6, 2016 at 11:45pm

▓▓▓▓▓▓▓▓▓ This isn't real. This is a satire piece. It's all intended
as a humorous slam at Trump.
Like · Reply · Message · October 7, 2016 at 1:11am

▓▓▓▓▓▓▓▓ Dont care about his tax returns. HOWEVER, HE
DID NOT "LOSE" THAT MONEY. HE OWNS PROPERTULIES,
EXPENSIVE PROPERTIES. IN THE 90S WHEN PROPERTY
VALUES DECLINED (& MANY lost big time on their homes.
Suddenly, their homes were worth 10s to 100s thousand dol...
See More
Like · Reply · Message · October 7, 2016 at 8:57pm

▓▓▓▓▓▓▓ Well we all know that Hillary was definitely truthful in
filing her taxes!!!
Like · Reply · Message · October 7, 2016 at 11:31pm

▓▓▓▓▓▓▓▓ Him and her both need go
Like · Reply · Message · October 8, 2016 at 9:13am

▓▓▓▓▓▓ This is satire, people! Relax.
Like · Reply · Message · October 8, 2016 at 10:24am

William Goodspeed I love all the responses, including photos
and cartoons, and even the ones that scold me. Thanks. BTW, this
is satire, but it's true that if you lose a lot of $ in a given year, you
can spread it out (if it's your money). It's perfectly legal and ethical
(if it's your money that you lost). I note that the media doesn't
seem willing to admit this.
Like · Reply · Message · October 8, 2016 at 3:47pm

████████████ They are asking him to step down and let pence run, pence has turned on him. 14 people said step down others are taking back endorsement so hes gone.

Like · Reply · Message · October 8, 2016 at 3:56pm

████████████ I hope all you beligerent, pseudo, social intellectuals all get your socialist feelings hurt after electing Obama and now thinking Hillary is our anointed savior!

Like · Reply · Message · October 8, 2016 at 4:55pm

William Goodspeed Keep the comments coming, social intellectuals and not. Good dialogue!

Like · Reply · Message · October 8, 2016 at 6:16pm

████████████ Trump is NOT a smooth butt kissing politician and I think it's time for a change away from professional establishment politicians.

Like · Reply · Message · October 8, 2016 at 6:22pm

████████████ Pence said he cannot control what trump says. They were supposed to go Wisconsin trump nor pence didn't sho so he has turned his back on trump.

Like · Reply · Message · October 8, 2016 at 6:33pm

████████████ Yea I can explain? But maybe you should ask Hilary and Warren Buffet how it works too! Because they have used it too!

Like · Reply · Message · October 8, 2016 at 9:22pm

████████████ Stop complaining about a person who followed are tax laws. Don't like it, change the laws.

Like · Reply · Message · October 9, 2016 at 7:18am

████████████ SO WHAT DIFFERENCE DOES IT MAKE;;; THAT WAS IN 1995, HOW STUPID CAN SOME PEOPLE GET!!!!!

Like · Reply · Message · October 7, 2016 at 1:24pm

██████████ This article is satire! Read to the end!

Like · Reply · Message · October 7, 2016 at 3:27pm

██████████ He seems to have forgot the 6 billon hillary lost

Like · Reply · Message · October 7, 2016 at 6:44pm

██████████ You mean the $6 billion that wasn't really lost?

Like · Reply · Message · October 7, 2016 at 8:54pm

██████████ Ya'll will believe anything, huh....

Like · Reply · Message · October 7, 2016 at 9:00pm

██████████ Snopes is the DNCs disinformation wing. They've
been exposed...

Like · Reply · Message · October 7, 2016 at 9:20pm

FORTY-NINE

Trump's 7-Month Itch
October 2016

Satirical Press International — It's 9 a.m. in New York, and CNN's elegant anchor, Carol Costello, opens her show:

Costello: Good morning! It's been quite a few days, culminating in the revealing of a 2005 recording and video of Donald Trump talking about groping women and being irresistible to them. To discuss this, we have a powerful panel this morning: Former Republican Congresswoman Michele Bachman, Dr. Gayle, a sex therapist from New York, and Tommy Ford, president of the Beta Chi fraternity at Western Carolina University. Good morning to all of you.

Group: Good morning, Carol.

Costello: Let's start with you, Representative Bachman. What do you say about Trump's 7-Month Itch — 7 months after Mr. Trump married the stunningly beautiful, nice and intelligent Melania, he talks freely about groping women and even used the 'P' word.

Bachman: This is another example of liberal media bias — he had been married 8 months.

Costello: Okay, so he got the 8-Month Itch. What do you think about a candidate talking that way?

Bachman: Bill Clinton said far worse on the golf course, and did worse, let's not forget. Plus, Mr. Trump apologized to 'anyone who might have been offended by his remarks.'

Costello: Except for you, I think he offended every woman on the planet, including his wonderful wife.

Bachman: Not to be difficult, Carol, but no one could know that.

Costello: Dr. Gayle, you deal with sex addiction all the time. What do you think of this?

Dr. Gayle: It's fairly common among about .1% of the male population, and it usually comes from a subconscious desire to compensate for personal shortcomings.

Costello: Like small hands?

Dr. Gayle: A good example, Carol.

Costello: What else do you think, Dr. Gayle?

Dr. Gayle: It's a little unusual because Mr. Trump was 58 years old at the time — this type of behavior usually burns out with age.

Costello: Interesting.

Dr. Gayle: And what's kind of impressive is that Everyday Cialis hadn't been invented yet.

Costello: Very interesting. Tommy, you live in your fraternity in North Carolina. What do you think about this?

Ford: When I first heard it on a local radio station, I got really worried.

Costello: Why?

Ford: Because I thought it might have been one of our freshmen pledges, which would have been totally inappropriate and immature, except the thing Trump said about Tic Tacs. I immediately started writing an apology letter to the university in my head.

Costello: What did you think when you learned it was Mr. Trump?

Ford: I was, like, totally relieved, but to be honest, I was shocked that a 58 year old man would talk that way.

Facebook Comments to Article:

▇▇▇▇▇▇▇ I guess what Trump said 11 years ago is more important than what Bill did 20 years ago. Liberism is a mental disorder.
Like · Reply · Message · October 10, 2016 at 11:25pm

▇▇▇▇▇▇▇▇ He said that happened years ago. And only Words. He is still light years better than the Clintons. He also apologized. Most people make mistakes. The Clintons commit horrible atrocities
Like · Reply · Message · October 11, 2016 at 12:21am

▇▇▇▇▇▇ Has anybody noticed the resemblance between his wife and Bruce Jenner
Like · Reply · Message · October 11, 2016 at 12:21am

▇▇▇▇▇▇ The lib/dem hypocrites who have no problem with Bill Clintons rapes... gays parading nude,men/boys in women/girls bathrooms, crude and vulgar rap lyrics,outfits and antics on stage...seem to have an issue with words they so often use..... go figure
Like · Reply · Message · October 11, 2016 at 12:31am

▇▇▇▇▇▇ Go scratch you own itch William you fake add POS
Like · Reply · Message · October 11, 2016 at 1:23am

▇▇▇▇▇▇▇ It's not like he's hiding emails..killing our citizens..it was more than 10yrs ago..get over it..
Like · Reply · Message · October 11, 2016 at 2:30am

▇▇▇▇▇▇ Not offended and don't care
Like · Reply · Message · October 11, 2016 at 5:51am

▮▮▮▮▮▮▮▮ Our "celebrity Republicans" currently are an insult to the party. They are terrified that Trump will be elected President. Undoubtedly, they are so scared that they do not care about our other political races or appointments to the Supreme Court.

Like · Reply · Message · October 11, 2016 at 8:29am

▮▮▮▮▮▮▮▮▮ He did not only liberal hypocrites 😊

Like · Reply · Message · October 11, 2016 at 9:30am

▮▮▮▮▮▮▮ If Trump would of said that lol

Like · Reply · Message · October 11, 2016 at 10:51am

▮▮▮▮▮▮ Trump paraded around the miss universe dressing room cause he was the boss

Like · Reply · Message · October 11, 2016 at 11:48am

▮▮▮▮▮▮ UMM.... NO... That's not what she should be concerned with. SHE SHOULD BE CONCERNED WITH KELLYANNE CONWAY'S REACTION!!! When this news hit. All of his surrogates male and female were immediately in front of a camera. But SHE DISAPPEARED!!! I put it to ...See More

Like · Reply · Message · October 11, 2016 at 12:26pm

▮▮▮▮▮▮▮▮ It's about time the Republicans nominated someone who can compete with Bill Clinton, JFK, LBJ and FDR in this department.

Like · Reply · Message · October 11, 2016 at 12:47pm

William Goodspeed Katie, is it something about men with celebrity status/power????????

Like · Reply · Message · October 11, 2016 at 6:49pm

▮▮▮▮▮▮▮▮▮ I don't get the connection. Is Bill Clinton running for office?

Like · Reply · Message · October 11, 2016 at 12:49pm

▮▮▮▮▮▮ "Last night a friend claimed that Donald Trump

wouldn't make a good president; he is brash, he is racist, he is a loudmouth; you know the normal things people learn to recite after being programmed by television news. The one I loved was that, "Trump i...*See More*

Like · Reply · Message · October 11, 2016 at 2:21pm

██████████ I believe it's important to point out, because many of y'all are too young to remember, that Hillary Clinton was once, just a short time ago, one of "rape cultures" biggest proponents, when she defended her husband against multiple rape accusers. Bill ...*See More*

Like · Reply · Message · October 11, 2016 at 2:21pm

██████████ If you all are so offended about what Trump said 10 yrs. ago and not what Clinton has done and will continue to do, you need a safe room.

Like · Reply · Message · October 11, 2016 at 2:34pm

██████████ Wonder if she'll divorce him after the election.

Like · Reply · Message · October 11, 2016 at 3:26pm

██████████ And this affects the issues facing our country how?

Like · Reply · Message · October 11, 2016 at 4:17pm

██████ It's nothing most men haven't bragged about at sometime in their life. Own up to it men

Like · Reply · Message · October 11, 2016 at 4:49pm

██████████ With all the wiki leaks confirming what we already know should be more of a concern but the media wants us to focus on this.

Like · Reply · Message · October 11, 2016 at 5:30pm

██████████ he ain't runnin for POPE.ASSHATS

Like · Reply · Message · October 11, 2016 at 10:20pm

██████████ Time to grow up children, in male dominated situations mining, logging, construction, military, etc, men talk like this, snowflakes. No big deal and more the norm than the exception. Far more offended by Clintons lawless actions spanning decades.

Like · Reply · Message · October 12, 2016 at 9:14am

██████████ Get off the Trump childish accusations .... What about slick Willie ?? He is guilty of rape and was impeached from the White House !! Hillary ' stands by her man ' and ridicules his accusers (not to mention, has no remorse for her abusive treatment of a 12 year old in her early lawyer days defending a brutal rape !!!)

Like · Reply · Message · October 12, 2016 at 9:41am

██████████ Oh no Trump offended me too...I just peed my pants ! Get a life knot head !!

Like · Reply · Message · October 12, 2016 at 12:45pm

████████ Wowza! You have some interesting "fans". It's amazing how many women condone this behavior and how Bill Clinton is their only defense. Keep up the good work. Bill!

Like · Reply · Message · October 12, 2016 at 1:38pm

████████ These people shut up and worry about more important world issues don't care what he did years ago and most of you did the same thing

Like · Reply · Message · October 12, 2016 at 1:41pm

███████ Get off it

Like · Reply · Message · October 12, 2016 at 2:00pm

█████████ I'm tired of people slinging mud

Like · Reply · Message · October 12, 2016 at 2:00pm

████████ I thought it was 7 year, not 7 month. Only proves he wanted to have sex with anyone but his pregnant wife.

Like · Reply · Message · October 12, 2016 at 4:40pm

██████████ TRUMP DID NOT OFFEND US MEN ARE MEN THEY ALL TALK CRAP SO DO WOMEN SO WHAT HE WILL MAKE A GREAT PRESIDENT AND MAKE AMERICA GREAT AGAIN HILLARY IS A LIAR AND MURDERER SO STICK IT TRUMP FOR PRESIDENT 2016 MANY SENATORS AND CONGRESSMAN HAVE TALKED...*See More*

Like · Reply · Message · October 12, 2016 at 7:17pm

██████████ We kill over 1,000,000 children a year in the United States. Hillary supports this killing. You don't have to answer to me for your vote. You have to answer to God.

Like · Reply · Message · October 13, 2016 at 3:09am

██████████ You offend me

Like · Reply · Message · October 13, 2016 at 10:38pm

██████████ I'm sorry but trump wasn't president through any of this..so it's called..his personal business..get over it ppl...this is nothing more than someone trying to stir up trouble

Like · Reply · Message · October 14, 2016 at 1:18am

██████████ Gish...the comments here...Thomas Jefferson had kids with his slaves and sold them...none of our presidents have been perfect but trump isn't even president n being condemned for what he's done in his private life..

Like · Reply · Message · October 14, 2016 at 1:28am

██████████ For 25 years I worked with men...in urology. Most of them over 60. The shrink needs to find more sources because I Can Tell you with a great deal of accuracy: they rarely "get over it".

Like · Reply · Message · October 14, 2016 at 5:51pm

██████████ Fake, fake, fake

Like · Reply · Message · October 14, 2016 at 7:37pm

FIFTY

Repeal the Women Vote (Party Like It's 1919)
October 2016

Satirical Press International — CNN's anchor, Carol Costello, opens her show from CNN studios in New York:

Costello: Good morning! With less than four weeks to go in the election, the furor over Donald Trump's 'locker room talk' has gripped the political landscape. Some Trump supporters have started a new movement: Repeal the 19th, referring to the 1920 Constitutional Amendment to grant women the right to vote. I'm here with Repeal the 19th spokesperson Mike Carlson. Good morning, Mr. Carlson.

Carlson: Good morning, Carol. Thanks for having me. It's important to shed light on this very important initiative.

Costello: Why repeal the 19th Amendment?

Carlson: It's simple Carol: women are the only thing standing between Donald Trump and the presidency. If only men could vote, Trump would win the Electoral College 350-188, a landslide.

Costello: Don't you think women will be upset about this?

Carlson: Nah, as one of our followers recently Tweeted: "Give out nice enough handbags and most broads would gladly trade their voting rights for one."

Costello: Did you really just say that?

Carlson: I just quoted one of our followers — look it up. We tell it like it is, Carol, just like Mr. Trump, which makes him great. Women don't have any interest in politics — they won't miss the vote.

Costello: But the Democratic candidate is a woman, Mr. Carlson.

Carlson: She just won't be able to vote for herself, no biggie.

Costello: I think you may be underestimating the negative reaction to this.

Carlson: We've done a lot of polling, and we think we have the votes to get this through before the election. Americans are really tired of the establishment. It would be the 28th Amendment to the U.S. Constitution — pretty exciting, I'd say.

Costello: You really think you have the support for this?

Carlson: Yeah, so much in fact that we may use the effort to tidy up the Constitution.

Costello: Tidy up?

Carlson: Yeah, like make background checks for firearm sales unconstitutional and other important housekeeping.

Costello: What housekeeping?

Carlson: Mandatory teaching of Genesis in high school, requiring NFL players to stand during the national anthem, legalizing torture — stuff that's been swept under the rug for too long.

Costello: Wow.

Carlson: Yeah, we're going to party like it's 1919.

Facebook Comments to Article:

███████████ OUR VOTES MATTER AND THEY ARE RUN
NING SCARED SHITLESS BECAUSE WE ARE ALL FOR TRUMP
HILLARY FOR THE DUMP TRUMP FOR PRESIDENT 2016
PENCE FOR VP 2016 GOD BLESS AMERICA
Like · Reply · Message · October 15, 2016 at 2:18pm

███████████ I think it's because a lot of women are changing
their mind and plan to vote for Hillary. I saw that on FOX. Makes
me happy because I'm with her.
Like · Reply · Message · October 15, 2016 at 3:55pm

████████████████ Women can vote ?
Like · Reply · Message · October 15, 2016 at 7:50pm

███████████ Excuse me Mr. Smith
Like · Reply · Message · October 15, 2016 at 8:51pm

█████████ I'm a woman but I don't want to Clinton present of me
as a woman.
Like · Reply · Message · October 15, 2016 at 8:53pm

███████████ The woman who fought for the right to vote were
Republicans
Like · Reply · Message · October 16, 2016 at 6:49am

███████████ Barefoot, pregnant and in the kitchen! The good
old days! Lol
Like · Reply · Message · October 16, 2016 at 8:40am

██████████████ I see someone sleeping in the dog house for
agreeing with this post! Lol....Y'all stay calm, Trumps got this!
Like · Reply · Message · October 16, 2016 at 11:17am

███████████ Interesting!
Like · Reply · Message · October 16, 2016 at 12:03pm

██████████████ Oh my...if all the world leaders were woman...there would only be wars over shoes...would that be so bad? 😊

Like · Reply · Message · October 16, 2016 at 12:37pm

████████ This is great, Bill! Scary thought that there are probably many Trump supporters who would vigorously support this!

Like · Reply · Message · October 16, 2016 at 1:24pm

█████████████ Who is William Goodspeed?

Like · Reply · Message · October 16, 2016 at 2:52pm

William Goodspeed Hi Jane - thanks for asking! I'm a reformed lawyer who spent over two decades as a senior executive in a variety of industries... an elaborate cover for my truth-seeking investigations into American life. ;) Learn more here... www. williamgoodspeed.com. 😊

Like · Reply · Message · October 16, 2016 at 2:52pm

████████████████ No comment other than TRUMP 2016-2024

Like · Reply · Message · October 16, 2016 at 3:49pm

███████████ I'm voting Evan mcmullen

Like · Reply · Message · October 16, 2016 at 4:18pm

██████████████ If Hillary wins the Democrat will destroy America if trump wins the democrat will the destroy America

Like · Reply · Message · October 16, 2016 at 11:20pm

████████████ I don't believe Trumps numbers with women anyway! I think women are smarter than this! Many Trump supporters are women! So why believe fake statistics? You cannot believe any poll results from them!

Like · Reply · Message · October 17, 2016 at 8:45am

██████████THE GOP DREAM!!!!!!!!

Like · Reply · Message · October 17, 2016 at 9:21am

█████████She is the Perfect Communist! Vote her out!!!!

Like · Reply · Message · October 17, 2016 at 9:44am

FIFTY-ONE

Clinton, Trump Debate Critical Issues
October 2016

Donald J. Trump ✔
@realDonaldTrump

Crooked Hillary Clinton deleted 33,000 e-mails AFTER they were subpoenaed by the United States Congress. Guilty - cannot run. Rigged system!

5:47 AM - 2 Nov 2016

4,174 replies 18,555 retweets 48,438 likes

Hillary Clinton ✔
@HillaryClinton

If Trump stands by what he said about women as "locker room talk," he's clearly not sorry.

5:24 AM - 10 Oct 2016

2,880 replies 11,897 retweets 25,630 likes

Satirical Press International — Veteran Fox anchor, Chris Wallace, opens television coverage of the third and final presidential debate. Facing candidates Trump and Clinton, he announces the debate format and ground rules to the expectant nation:

Wallace: Good evening from Las Vegas, host of the final presidential debate in the 2016 campaign. In response to the rambling rancor of previous debates, the Commission on Presidential Debates has altered the format of tonight's contest. Sitting behind me are 500 American citizens representing a cross-section of America, all different ages, ethnic groups, socio-economic status, genders, sexual orientations and political parties.

Wallace: For the past three hours, this group has participated in an unprecedented form of debate democracy. We started with 30 issues facing our country, and by process of elimination voting, ended with two for tonight's debate. Domestic issues considered included the huge federal debt, the future of Medicare, gun violence, pantsuits, tax abuse, Rosie O'Donnell and immigration. On the international side, we had ISIS, the Syrian conflict, Russian aggression, a nuclear North Korea and Vladimir Putin, friend or foe?

Wallace: Neither of the candidates knows the results of this voting, and I'm pleased to announce that this group of Americans behind me has voted and decided that the two most important issues facing our nation are: 1. The sexual past of Donald Trump, including the so-called locker room talk, and 2. Secretary Clinton's email controversy. We thank the group for their thoughtful efforts and now turn to the candidates:

Wallace: Mr. Trump, you won the coin toss, so we start with you. Over the past two weeks, several women have claimed that you performed unwanted touching and kissing on them. What do you say to them?

Trump: They are — sniff — liars, all of them, — sniff — believe me. Take one look, one look. Do you — sniff — really think I'd be tempted by any of them? Miss Piggy would — sniff — be a better catch, no offense to Kermit. It's not credible; it's all made up by the liberal media. They are very dishonest, bad people.

Wallace: They all just made it up by themselves?

Trump: No, they — sniff — had help, believe me. The New York Times has many, many writers who — sniff — are out to get me, just like CNN. They helped them create the stories, trust me folks.

Wallace: So you're denying the charges?

Trump: Absolutely. In any event, it's nothing — sniff — compared to what Bill Clinton did while he was in office, nothing, trust me. Apparently, he got tired of Hillary's pantsuits, believe me, not that I blame him.

Wallace: Secretary Clinton, do you have any comment on the pantsuit issue?

Clinton: My pantsuits are not an appropriate topic for this debate, and it shows Mr. Trump's misogyny. You won't hear me talking about his hair or orange complexion — that would not be presidential. In fact, I have a plan for ending locker room talk — you can see the details on Hillary. com. Under my watch, we will end locker room talk once and for all!

(*Huge applause from audience*)

Wallace: May I remind the audience that no cheering is allowed. Let's go to the next question. Secretary Clinton, you deleted about 33,000 emails from your private server. What was on those emails?

Clinton: Mostly Chelsea's wedding plans. As you know, Chris, the parents of the bride have the lion's share of wedding planning.

Wallace: 33,000 seems like a lot.

Clinton: One of my biggest faults, and I admit it freely here tonight because I am human after all, is I'm a perfectionist. I will not rest until everything is right, for Chelsea's wedding and America!

(*Huge applause*)

Clinton: Just like my poor overworked father who trimmed curtains every night, but gave me an appreciation of the regular American.

(*Huge applause*)

Wallace: Again, may I remind the audience to hold their applause until the end of the debate. Secretary Clinton, the FBI said your private server housed material labeled 'Classified' and even sent those materials to others on an unsecured line.

Clinton: I've been to 112 countries, Chris, negotiated peace agreements, hostage releases and other important matters, all while Mr. Trump let his fingers do the talking, to use an old Yellow Pages jingle.

Wallace: You didn't answer the question: did you send classified emails?

Clinton: I regret very much using my private server, but I wanted to have everything on one device. When you're negotiating a peace deal in the Middle East and the florist for Chelsea's wedding needs a decision, you can't be flipping back and forth.

Wallace: But did you send classified emails?

Clinton: They weren't labeled 'Classified' — they just had the letter 'C'. I thought the C stood for 'Cool', meaning it was cool to send. How was I supposed to know?

Wallace: You were the Secretary of State.

Clinton: If you and the press want to play 'gotcha,' have at it, but America wants to return to the key issues of this campaign, Mr. Trump's groping and locker room talk!

Wallace: Thank you, Secretary Clinton, Mr. Trump for a great debate.

(*Huge applause and whistling while the candidates wave*)

CNN's Jake Tapper sits with NBC's Lester Holt and ABC's George Stephanopoulos in a studio.

Stephanopoulos: I think Secretary Clinton may have dealt a knock out blow to Mr. Trump tonight. Her announcement about ending locker room talk was political brilliance.

Holt: She had that arrow waiting in her quiver, that's for sure, but I thought Mr. Trump handled himself very presidentially tonight. His answers about groping showed more presidential presence and temperament than we've seen from the candidate before, even though the sniffles still seem to dog him.

Stephanopoulos: Well, it is the beginning of the cold and flu season.

Tapper: It will be interesting to hear how the American public viewed the contest. We haven't had a poll in 12 hours, and we could see some seismic movement after this contest.

Facebook Comments to Article:

████████████ Trump is the sniffer.....
Like · Reply · Message · October 19, 2016 at 5:53pm

████████████████ And Obama was the admitted cocaine sniffer. Hillary was the one who had her handler arrange sexual liaisons with men AND women.
Like · Reply · Message · October 19, 2016 at 7:52pm

██████████████ VOTE TRUMP AND PENCE IN NOVEMBER !!!!!!!!!!!!!!!!!!!
Like · Reply · Message · October 19, 2016 at 8:19pm

██████████████ What debate was Goodspeed watching? !? Trump didn't say anything about miss piggy or Hillary's ugly overpriced pantsuit!
Like · Reply · Message · October 20, 2016 at 8:06am

William Goodspeed To be honest, the blog came out before the debate, and was meant to point out how this election has not focused on the big issues.
Like · Reply · Message · October 20, 2016 at 11:20am

██████████████ Donna they are just a bunch of ignorant liberals that refuse to see facts and publish what will help clinton get elected. Want America to become a third world country

Like · Reply · Message · October 20, 2016 at 10:04am

██████████ IT SHOWS SHE WAS CHEATING AGAIN WITH HER BEING TALKED TO BY OTHERS CAUSE WHEN THE DEBATE A GUY RUSHES OVER AND PICKS IT UP OFF HER PODIUM ! SHE CAN'T DO A DEBATE WITHOUT IT CAUSE HER HEAD IS GONE TO PARKINSON'S ! AND WHERE WAS THAT DRUG TEST TRUMP WANTED SHE WOULDN'T AGREE TO IT WHY ????????

Like · Reply · Message · October 20, 2016 at 11:08am

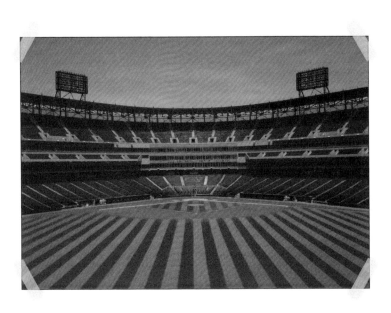

FIFTY-TWO

Cubs Series Win Ominous Sign for Clinton
November 2016

Hillary Clinton ✔
@HillaryClinton

They did it! 108 years later and the drought is finally over.
Way to make history, @Cubs. #FlyTheW -H

10:06 PM - 2 Nov 2016

2,846 replies 14,718 retweets 59,584 likes

Donald J. Trump ✔
@realDonaldTrump

I hear the Rickets family, who own the Chicago Cubs, are
secretly spending $'s against me. They better be careful, they
have a lot to hide!

6:42 AM - 22 Feb 2016

3,740 replies   9,340 retweets   16,467 likes

Satirical Press International — In the wee hours this morning, the
Chicago Cubs ended 108 years of futility with an extra-inning victory in
Game 7 of the World Series. The victory sent shock waves throughout
America and around the world.

In South Chicago, gunfire erupted soon after the final out. Police originally thought it was a long overdue celebration of a world championship, but later determined that it was another outbreak of gang warfare.

A man in Kalamazoo, Michigan captured what so many Americans felt about this milestone: "This is maybe the greatest thing since the U.S. hockey team beat the Russians in 1980. Today, I learned the meaning of America." When reminded by an SPI reporter that the Cleveland Indians were from the United States, the man said, "But it's close to Canada, right?"

Others predicted the unlikely Cubs comeback was a sign of a Trump upset on Election Day. "If the Cubs can come back from down 3-1 and end their 108-year drought," one Chicagoan said, "then by golly, why can't a man with bad hair who offends almost everyone become President. This is America."

Back in Cleveland, fans lamented the Indians' failure to hold a 3-1 lead with the last two games at home. "It's the biggest Great Lakes disaster since the wreck of the Edmund Fitzgerald," decried one man. "Gordon Lightfoot will probably write a ballad about it."

Overseas, the reaction to the Cub victory was instant. Kim Jong Un of North Korea, a frustrated longtime Cubs fan, immediately ordered his military to set off 'the mother of all fireworks displays, including a couple nukes.' In Tehran, the Ayatollah appeared on national Iranian television to comment on the World Series. He captured Iranian sentiment very poignantly: "Holy Cow! Go Cubs and Death to America!"

During the post-game celebration with champagne and beer, the Cubs received a congratulatory phone call from Russian President Vladimir Putin, who invited the entire team to a celebration at the Kremlin. "Now that's strong leadership," commented Donald Trump during an event in Jacksonville, Florida.

Back in the clubhouse, Game 7 starter and Ivy League graduate Kyle Hendricks summed up the celebration: "Everyone was yelling and screaming, drunk, drooling and covered with beer. It was a lot like Dartmouth on a Saturday night."

FIFTY-THREE

Trump Upsets Clinton in Landslide!
November 8, 2016

 Donald J. Trump ✔
@realDonaldTrump

In addition to winning the Electoral College in a landslide, I won the popular vote if you deduct the millions of people who voted illegally

12:30 PM - 27 Nov 2016

50,661 replies 53,434 retweets 162,402 likes

Satirical Press International — For the second time in a week, the world was rocked by a massive upset. Less than 6 days after the Cubs extinguished its longtime curse, Republican Candidate Donald Trump defeated Democrat Hillary Clinton in the U.S. Presidential Election.

"It wasn't an upset," responded Kelly Ann Conway, a spokesperson from the Trump Campaign, to a question posed by SPI's Sophie Garibaldi. "The only reason people think it was an upset was because the biased media had falsified the polls all along with fake news. We knew all along that a convincing victory was in the making."

Garibaldi continued: "So, you're saying all of the polls leading up to the election were wrong?"

"They all came from the media, which are liberal and have a leftist agenda," Conway responded.

"Even Fox News?"

"Fox is the most objective, behind Steve Bannon's Breitbart News Network of course."

"Back to your statement, Ms. Conway," Garibaldi continued. "You're saying the election was a landslide?"

"Absolutely. Despite the liberal news media and its fake news, Donald Trump dominated the contest."

"Really?"

"Clearly. It was the largest Electoral College victory since Reagan," Conway answered.

"Except for Barack Obama's two elections and Bush Senior in 1988," Garibaldi responded.

"Those are just alternative facts invented by the media — President-Elect Trump trounced Secretary Clinton."

"Is it fair to say he trounced Secretary Clinton when he lost the popular vote by two million votes?" Garibaldi asked.

"Clearly another invention of the liberal press. If you don't count the 3-5 million illegal votes, President-Elect Trump won the popular vote."

"Really?"

"Absolutely. Also, the only reason we lost New Hampshire is that liberals bussed people in to vote illegally from left wing Massachusetts," Conway snapped.

"What facts do you have to support these allegations of illegal voting?"

"Well, for example, several on the President-elect's staff are registered in more than one state," Conway barked.

"So you're saying that because people on the President-Elect's own staff could vote illegally is evidence that millions did so, all in favor of Secretary Clinton?"

"It's a well known fact, Ms. Garibaldi. I've read stories from your network for more than a year, and you clearly publish fake news. You need to listen to us and realize there are alternative facts."

"Thank you, Ms. Conway, and good luck on the transition."

Donald J. Trump ✅
@realDonaldTrump

I will be asking for a major investigation into VOTER FRAUD, including those registered to vote in two states, those who are illegal and....

4:10 AM - 25 Jan 2017

45,383 replies   26,460 retweets   131,937 likes

Donald J. Trump ✅
@realDonaldTrump

The same people who did the phony election polls, and were so wrong, are now doing approval rating polls. They are rigged just like before.

5:11 AM - 17 Jan 2017

28,811 replies   24,898 retweets   108,454 likes

ABOUT THE AUTHOR

When people see this picture, they always ask the same thing: "What's with the hat?" It's an excellent question, albeit obvious. Unfortunately, the hat, a 1970s vintage agricultural model, was only loaned to me--the farm wouldn't even entertain my generous offer to buy it.

The farm did, however, graciously give me the arm sleeve as a souvenir. After several cleanings, it now hangs decoratively on our family room wall. One of the kids wanted to use it as a stocking for Christmas, but sometimes, you gotta draw the line.

Whenever I'm asked what inspired me to write *Alternative Facts*, I return to the experience of my first pregnancy test on a dairy cow. She was a terrific sport, though she had to get doped up first (see syringe in picture), not that I blame her. It wasn't all fun and games for me either, as my expression shows. But I must say, it was far more enjoyable than the 2016 American presidential election. My bovine friend, who admittedly had a more challenging role in the process, said it reminded her of being on the wrong end of a Donald Trump Tweet.

Just an aside: this experience inspired the creation of a bovine pregnancy test developed by IDEXX Laboratories, a veterinarian biotech company in Maine. You can't pick it up at a Walgreen's and it doesn't have a smiley face for a positive test, but it's a lot easier on the arms (and nose).

And before anyone gets going on dairy cows being un-American, immoral and promiscuous, remember that without them, we wouldn't have Velveeta (I think).